THE JOYSTRINGS

THE STORY OF THE SALVATION ARMY POP GROUP

THE JOYSTRINGS

THE STORY OF THE SALVATION ARMY POP GROUP

SYLVIA DALZIEL

SHIELD
BOOKS

© The Salvation Army
United Kingdom Territory with
the Republic of Ireland

The Joystrings: The Story of The Salvation Army Pop Group
Sylvia Dalziel

First published in 2013 by
Shield Books
© The Salvation Army
United Kingdom Territory with the Republic of Ireland
101 Newington Causeway, London SE1 6BN

ISBN 978-0-85412-906-5

Book Editor: John Mitchinson
Text Editor: Bruce Tulloch
Design: Rob Gould

CREDITS: ABC TV (p.30, bottom left and bottom right); Braintree and Witham Times (p.69; p.73); Daily Mail (p.81, top
left); Daily Mirror (p.75, main; p.95); Getty Images (p.24); Leslie Priest/AP/Press Association Images (p.67, main); Radio
Times (p.83; p.108); Salvation Army International Heritage Centre (p.89, left); TV Times (p.49, bottom; p.51, centre);
Vauxhall Motor Company (p.29, top right). Used with permission.

'Visionary, groundbreaking and courageous.

'It was back in the days when guitars in church, let alone music with a beat, were for many a definite no-no. But there, in the forefront of Christian evangelism, even with a track in the secular charts, were The Salvation Army's "Joystrings", proving that the Devil certainly didn't have all the good music!

'Thank you Joy, and all those who dared go where others were much too cautious, for making it easier for me and for countless other Christian musicians who have come since, to minister musically in the only way we know how!'

Sir Cliff Richard

July 2013

SINGLES

It's an Open Secret/
Set the World a-Singing (RZ501, 1964)

A Million Songs/Joshua (RZ503, 1964)

A Starry Night/Now I Know (RZ504, 1964)

All Alone/He Cares (RZ505, 1965)

The Only One/You're Welcome (RZ506, 1965)

EPS

The Joy Strings (ERZ8255, 1965)

Have Faith In God (ERZ8252, 1965)

Christmas with The Joy Strings
(ERZ8260, 1965)

Joy Strings Abroad (ERZ8261, 1966)

The Song Break (ERZ8264, 1967)

ALBUMS

Well Seasoned (SLRZ4016, 1966)

Carols Around the World (SLRZ4108, 1967)

THE JOYSTRINGS

MUSIC RELEASES

CONTENTS

ACKNOWLEDGEMENTS

THE JOYSTRINGS

I WOULD LIKE TO EXPRESS MY WARMEST GRATITUDE TO THOSE WHO HAVE supported me throughout the writing of this book. Firstly, to Hazel, the Joystrings' 'number one fan', without whose meticulous recording of events I would have struggled, and to John Mitchinson, my Book Editor, for the energy, diligence and enthusiasm he has poured into this project. Naturally the finished product relied enormously on the text editing skills of Bruce Tulloch and the creative book design of Rob Gould – thank you both! To Joy, Wycliffe and Liz, who have often been on the end of the phone when I have needed a listening ear and some further words of encouragement to continue the project, and to General John Larsson (Retired) who so kindly agreed to write the Foreword. My thanks must also go to The Salvation Army's Publishing Department in the United Kingdom for agreeing to underwrite and market this production.

And finally to my husband, Peter, for the time he has given, not only to sorting and researching with me the photographic material, but also for his patience and understanding when I have 'disappeared' into the study for days at a time working on the book.

Thank you all.

Sylvia Dalziel

FOREWORD

THE JOYSTRINGS

LITTLE DID NEWLY ELECTED GENERAL FREDERICK COUTTS KNOW WHEN he got home from his first press conference after entering office on 23 November 1963 that some off-the-cuff words of his had started a revolution!

What he said that day gave birth to the Joystrings – and when the Joystrings appeared on the scene a revolution began that, in the words of EMI record producer Walter Ridley, changed the face of religious music for ever.

The impact of the Joystrings, with their new sound and their new way of reaching the young, was astounding. The press could not get enough of them. Television and radio queued up to feature them. Great crowds gathered to hear them wherever they appeared. Hundreds of young people were won for the Lord.

Most of the saints thanked the Lord for this stunning breakthrough in Salvation Army music-making and outreach, but some were not sure that God approved of electric guitars in his service, especially at full volume. General Coutts had a reassuring word for them. 'The Joystrings,' he said, 'exist for sinners, not the saints.'

With *The Joystrings: The Story of The Salvation Army Pop Group* we at last have a full record of those amazing five years during which the Christian music scene was lit up by the Joystrings. Sylvia Dalziel tells the story from a unique vantage point – from the inside. We not only follow the group on its journeys, but get to know the members as individuals and learn of their thoughts and feelings. We watch the group coping with hard knocks as well as rejoicing in triumphs. We see a team honing not only its creative skills but also its ability to communicate the gospel. Finally we hear Joy Webb herself reflecting on those iconic years. And above everything else, we sense the Lord's hand in it all.

This book, with its fascinating text and memorable photo images, together with the two CDs of original Joystrings recordings – *Joystrings Restrung* and *The Joystrings Christmas Collection* – bring to life again a remarkable chapter in the history of The Salvation Army. Thank you, Sylvia Dalziel, and everyone else involved. As we draw inspiration from the past we look with even greater confidence to the future.

John Larsson
GENERAL (RETIRED)

July 2013

INTRODUCTION

THE JOYSTRINGS

IT IS 50 YEARS SINCE THE SALVATION ARMY POP GROUP, THE JOYSTRINGS, came into being, in November 1963. Some internet sites state that it was this group that set the ball rolling as far as modern church music is concerned. Indeed, the late Walter Ridley – the Joystrings' record producer – wrote in 1973 that when the Joystrings walked through the doors of EMI's Abbey Road recording studios in St John's Wood, London, the face of religious music changed for ever.

This book is my story of how the group was born and what happened during almost five years of its existence. Since I'm the one telling this story, and I was a member of the group for most of that time – and I'm married to the bass guitarist of the group – the story naturally includes an amount of individual reflection of all that happened. In fact, there are moments in the narrative when I reveal something of how I felt about the challenges which were thrust upon me personally during those years.

The final chapter is contributed by Joy Webb. It was under her leadership that the group functioned and under whose directive engagements were scheduled, and this chapter gives the reader a chance to look behind the scenes and on to the real arena of battle. Joy writes with a frankness and honesty which confirm the fact that the Joystrings happening at all was an absolute miracle!

The book also records for posterity a chronological history of all that took place during this time, and so inevitably schedules and travel details play a vital part in the story. Anyone who has ever been involved in group work will know that such detailed explanation is helpful for understanding the lifestyle that is compelled upon group members and the physical and emotional pressure under which they work on a day-to-day basis. This is not always easily appreciated by those who are not 'in the business'.

My story of the Joystrings follows the production of two compact discs of the best known of the group's music of the Sixties. These digitally enhanced recordings, *Joystrings Restrung* and *The Joystrings Christmas Collection*, are now available for those who want to indulge in a bit of nostalgia and assess for themselves just how radical this new religious pop sound of the early Sixties was.

I have been able to record the story of the group's work so concisely due to the diligence of one or two people whose interest in the group at the time led them to keep and catalogue programmes, press cuttings, photographs and other memorabilia to do with the Joystrings. Of course, each group member kept their own albums – though I would hazard a guess that, because of our schedules at the time, none of us was able to keep a perfect record of everything. In particular, I have been able to supplement what the members have between us, with the very generous donation of albums of memorabilia from someone who was at the time our 'number one fan', and much more diligent in her recording of events than we in the group ever were.

It is important to remember that the Sixties was the era of 'liberation'. There was, especially among young people, an explosion of free expression in the arts, in fashion, in the media. In fact, in every area of life there was a feeling of wanting to move on and change. Such feelings could be understood following the years of austerity, rationing and rebuilding after the Second World War. So in a sense, Britain, along with the rest of the world, was poised and open to new ideas wherever they came from.

However, the birth of the Joystrings was not engineered. There was no plan for a Salvation Army pop group. There wasn't even a seed thought on the subject! One hopes that every denomination of the Christian Church is always considering how best to reach out and communicate the gospel message in its everyday ministry. But thoughts of a Christian pop group going into nightclubs, appearing regularly on television, recording in the same studios as the Beatles, and the release of full-time ordained people for such ministry, had never been considered. It simply happened, initially because of a very wise Salvation Army international leader thinking 'outside the box' and allowing what came next to evolve naturally.

None of us who were at different times selected to be members of the group had any special spiritual prowess. We had not even learned the rudiments of being full-time ministers. Some of us, in our late teens, were barely out of school. So don't think as you read the story that there was any great spiritual preparation to the formation of the Joystrings – not on earth, anyway. But even as the story moves through the five years of our existence we have to realise that, if we as young people were lacking in spiritual skill, there were spiritual giants all around the world who were praying for the success of our ministry. Our testimony is that we were constantly buoyed up by their belief in our mission, and together with our own faltering efforts in preparation before any event, we knew that we were strengthened by a power beyond ourselves.

The story of the Joystrings is a miracle story, really, and one which could only have been planned in Heaven. Could it happen again? I leave you to answer that question after you have read the book. It is obvious now, of course, that the Joystrings group was specifically *for such a time*. However, we must believe there are other God-ordained plans in the offing, just waiting for the right moment. God help us to be ready to embrace them and have the faith and *courage* to go with them!

'Joy writes with a frankness and honesty which confirm the fact that the Joystrings happening at all was an absolute miracle!'

TIME & TIDE

JOHN O' LONDON'S

30 JANUARY—5 FEBRUARY 1964   ONE SHILLING WEEKLY

Guitars as well as Big Drums

Salvation Army's General Coutts —3,000,000 soldiers behind him

1

HOW
IT ALL
BEGAN

A CHANCE REMARK BY GENERAL Frederick Coutts, newly elected International Leader of The Salvation Army, on 23 November 1963 in his first press interview, began it all.

He was asked by some journalist what new perspective he would bring to The Salvation Army during his term of office. The General turned the question back to the reporters: 'What do *you* think we should be doing to communicate with people today?' The response was immediate – 'Communication today is through pop music with guitars – you know, the Beatles sound!'

'Well,' said the General, 'it should be possible to take the gospel message to coffee bars with electric guitars if this proves to be an effective method!'

Seizing on the General's word, the next day the press went to town. Cartoonists had a field day. One of them depicted a group holding a meeting outdoors – bandsmen retreating with brass instruments under their arms while usurpers plugged their guitars into the street lighting. The whole idea of The Salvation Army using electric guitars had obviously captured the imagination of the press, and naturally they wanted to see and hear what the Army had to offer in the way of a 'pop group'. Surprised staff in the General's office at Salvation Army Headquarters referred the press to the Principal of the Army's vocational training college in Denmark Hill, South London – at least there they would find a substantial nucleus of students (known as cadets in The Salvation Army) who could sing, and one or two might even play a guitar.

A college staff member, Captain Joy Webb, a house officer, tutor and leader of the girls' choir, was a guitar player herself, as well as an accomplished pianist, and had an aptitude for anything musical. So she was summoned to the Principal's office and asked to get some kind of group together – quickly – for a photographic session to satisfy the press. All this was easy enough – select some girls from the choir, then take them to Westminster to find a suitable background for the photo session. *Time & Tide* magazine had them photographed outside 10 Downing Street, the British Prime Minister's official residence, for its front cover, while other agency photographers favoured the background of the Houses of Parliament.

The photographs appeared in the next day's national newspapers, and everyone thought that would be it. The pictures were out, and the fuss would die down. But far from it – now people wanted to *hear* the music!

The Canadian Broadcasting Company was one of the first media companies to make a bid to film the Salvation Army 'group' singing 'pop music'. This seemed a reasonable request since the Training Principal, Commissioner Clarence Wiseman, was a Canadian. So Joy Webb had to prepare an arrangement of an up-tempo Salvation Army chorus, and teach a couple of men cadets who owned acoustic guitars how to play them, all as quickly as possible!

And so it was that Peter Dalziel and Bill Davidson were brought in to join 'the girls'. The song was learned, there were good voices to sing it, and they presented a reasonable sound for an impromptu performance. More than reasonable: it was so acceptable that there quickly followed an invitation from the BBC's *Tonight* TV programme, hosted by Cliff Michelmore, for the ad hoc group to perform on the show, together with news clips from their outside broadcast in Brixton Market, South London. At the end of the transmission, the BBC's switchboard was jammed with calls from people asking to see more of this Salvation Army group. Within a few weeks these swinging Salvationists were on television for the second time, again on the popular *Tonight* programme. It was 14 January – roughly six weeks after the chance remark of General Coutts to the press to 'see what we can do'!

Such out-of-the-blue, raw, unsolicited exposure for these young people started something which took The Salvation Army, the Church and the rest of the world by surprise. All kinds of invitations suddenly poured in for this group – which was still nameless – to appear in their club or at their venue. Recording company EMI offered to make a test recording in their Abbey Road studios in London. EMI had for many years been recording Salvation Army brass bands under the label Regal Zonophone.

Obviously some serious dialogue had to take place between the Training Principal and the General. Cadets Brenda Alexander, Thelma Adams and Lilian Boot, the three girl vocalists finally selected from the group of girls first photographed, together with

Above: Outside broadcast in Brixton Market

13

Peter Dalziel and Bill Davidson, were after all students, and as such had a curriculum to follow and grades to achieve in order to be ordained as full-time Salvation Army officers (ministers). On the other hand, this was a door of opportunity to evangelise in an unprecedented way – which was where all the cadets' training and studying was intended to be heading anyway – and it was too good to disregard. In fact, this was a God-given opening for The Salvation Army to communicate to the world in a bang-up-to-date style.

LET'S RUN WITH IT

ONCE again Salvation Army leaders were prepared to take an inspired risk. They decided to run with it and see what would happen. The group, as it was then, was initially called exactly what it was – The International Training College String Band Rhythm Group – something of a mouthful! It would not be until some weeks later that the name 'Joystrings' came about. In addition to the girl vocalists, Joy, Peter and Bill on guitars and vocals, Joy enlisted the help of a good friend, Wycliffe Noble, who was a Salvationist and professional architect and also a drummer. She also asked a fellow staff member of the college, Captain Handel Everett, to play a string bass which they borrowed from a nearby school to make up the rhythm section. That made eight members in all – quite a line-up!

Permission was granted for the cadets to work their college lessons alongside invitations for the group. What was now needed was some new song material. This task initially fell to Joy, the co-ordinator of the group, and it wasn't long before she had a couple of songs ready for rehearsal – 'It's an Open Secret' and 'We're Going to Set the World a-Singing'. It was these early days of 'where needs must' which launched Joy into what became a lifetime of prolific songwriting and which continues to go on blessing people around the world, and which she has written about in her book *Bridge of*

Songs. At that time, the Church was still very much held in the grip of sacred hymns, many with the language of a bygone age. They were beautiful words, solidly doctrinal themes and in intensely poetic language, but what did they communicate to the man in the street?

Joy confesses to being deeply challenged by the problem. She tells the story of how, one Monday morning, when the cadets met together in their assembly hall at the college, she heard the Training Principal's wife read from the Apostle Paul's letter to the Colossians in the translation by Dr James Moffatt. One particular verse jumped out at her – chapter 1, verse 26 – and the title of her first Joystrings song came – 'that open secret…'

> 'One particular verse jumped out at her – chapter 1, verse 26 – and the title of her first Joystrings song came – "that open secret…"'

A NAME IS BORN

SHORTLY before the group went along to the Abbey Road studios to record these two new songs, Joy was invited to EMI House at 20 Manchester Square, London, to discuss some legal issues regarding the recording. The discussion was to take place over lunch with Abbey Road's repertoire manager at the time, Robert Dockerill.

Joy remembers that they were walking down the stairs inside EMI House together when they bumped into George Martin, the Beatles' recording manager from EMI Abbey Road. Robert was just about to introduce George to Joy, when George grabbed the initiative, thrust forward his hand and said, 'Joy Webb – Salvation Army!' Obviously the initial press publicity had made its mark.

Over lunch Robert discussed naming the group – 'Something far removed from the world of brass bands,' he said, and then added, 'In fact, something to do with strings. What about "Joystrings"?'

Joy was uncertain, for obvious reasons. 'Does it have to be *Joy* strings?' she said. But Robert Dockerill was adamant and went on to explain his reasoning. 'The New Testament is full of the joy of being a Christian. And since the group's music expresses this fact, the name "Joystrings" fits perfectly.' So, a name was born.

HITTING THE CHARTS

A FEW weeks later, the recording that the group thought was simply a test recording was actually released as a single by EMI. It immediately soared into the record charts. The HMV sales shop in Oxford Street, London, at that time the biggest in Britain, ran its own chart based on current sales, and on 14 February 1964 'It's an Open Secret' was in at number 16 – quite a Valentine's Day gift for The Salvation Army! It made number 32 in the national charts (although some newspapers claimed it made number 26) and stayed in for seven weeks.

In the early Sixties, airtime could be bought by the UK record

Top: First group photo at the training college
Left: First use of the name 'the Joystrings'

15

companies for promotion on Radio Luxembourg, which had a medium-wave and short-wave service beamed directly at Britain. Among other programmes, EMI controlled the *Friday Spectacular*, a ticketed one-hour show broadcast by Radio Luxembourg but recorded live at EMI House theatre studio. It was a pop disc-plugging programme, and featured current top EMI artists such as the Beatles, Cliff Richard, Gene Pitney, Bobby Vee and Jess Conrad.

When the new Salvation Army group arrived for their performance on the show, they were greeted by 100 screaming teenagers who had managed to get tickets. Interviewed by Shaw Taylor, who, it is recorded, was the first DJ to interview the Beatles, Joy explained that the aim of the group was to bring the gospel message to people who wouldn't normally consider going to church. Shaw Taylor responded by saying he saw this as a natural extension for an Army which is renowned for always being in the front line. The storm of applause which greeted the group at the end of their live performance of 'It's an Open Secret' was overwhelming, prompting a 'Wow!' from the compère.

This public appearance was quickly followed by an invitation for Joy to be interviewed by Jimmy Young on his BBC radio show *Saturday Special*. There she talked about the Joystrings and their first recording which had gone straight into the charts.

IT'S ABOUT MINISTRY

THE group's first real public appearance was at a special Salvation Army meeting held in Camberwell, South London. The location was not surprising, really, because the old Camberwell Salvation Army hall was used every Thursday by cadets and staff of the International Training College for their holiness meeting, a very important part of the programme for cadets for their future evangelistic ministry.

Camberwell's old hall, it could be said, was ideal for music presentation. It had a large arena and the platform (stage) was in tiered levels from which the Joystrings were to make their first public outing. Sixty per cent of that audience were teenagers, and the presentation ended with words of appeal to embrace the

Christian faith. During the prayer time which followed, many young people moved forward to the front of the platform to signify their desire to know more about God. This memorable evening set the pattern for all future concert 'performances' by the Joystrings.

THE BLUE ANGEL

WHO would have believed that a group which sprang from nowhere, in the space of a few weeks would have been invited to play on the cabaret floor of the prestigious Blue Angel nightclub in Mayfair, London? And not just once, but for three successive nights!

The Salvation Army was actually no stranger to clubbing. For years Salvation Army cadets from the college had gone out under the guidance of well-experienced officers to practise their developing skills in evangelism among the people who frequented the clubs, sex shops and drinking saloons of London's infamous Soho. It has always been the practice of the Army to take its ministry to wherever people are. And many people will remember how, all over the country, it was not unusual to hear a Salvation Army girl, or sometimes a lad, sing a song in a pub when doing their rounds selling *The War Cry*, the Army's evangelistic newspaper.

But this invitation for the group actually to take part in cabaret to a very sophisticated audience was something else. This was where professional artistes were invited, and photographs of former performers at the club hung on the walls as a reminder to those who visited that only the best of stars performed here. What would Marlene Dietrich, who gazed from her picture with mild amazement, have thought of these raw young musicians who sang about the love of God?

Noel Harrison and Rex, his famous film-star father, were both present on the first night presentation of the Joystrings. In fact, Noel compèred the evening.

There were many clients who stayed on in those early morning hours after the Joystrings' performance, talking with the group members, sharing confidences, seeking spiritual advice and asking soul-searching questions. One man who passed over a menu to be autographed admitted that he used to be a Salvationist himself, and that evening had made him remember and rethink what he was doing with his life.

So even in the very early days, when these young Salvationists were as bewildered as anyone else about how quickly things were happening which were totally unplanned and unimagined, it seemed that an infinitely greater power was in control. None of what happened during the five years of the Joystrings' existence could have been achieved without this spiritual force. We, as Christians, acknowledge this as the power of God's Holy Spirit driving forward and sweeping away convention and established protocol in order to proclaim the gospel. I believe I have read much of the same in the history of the Early Church!

'The storm of applause which greeted the group at the end of their live performance of "It's an Open Secret" was overwhelming, prompting a "Wow!" from the compère'

Clockwise from top right: First public appearance at Camberwell; The Blue Angel Nightclub; The *Friday Spectacular* live show

Above: The new line-up in Wycliffe's MG

2

LOOK
TO THE
FUTURE

THE JOYSTRINGS

IT WAS *NEVER* ENVISAGED THAT THE life of the Joystrings would last anything like five years. In the beginning it was simply a response to a press call to prove that The Salvation Army was 'with it' in terms of the ways in which the Organisation could evangelise.

Brenda, Lilian and Thelma were rapidly moving towards the day of their commissioning and ordination in the Royal Albert Hall with all the other cadets of their year. Their chosen vocation was as full-time Salvation Army officers, and they would receive appointments which could be anywhere in the country, or even beyond. That being the case, the Training Principal and those staff members involved with this pop group had to decide how to handle the list of invitations which had come in for them to 'perform'. By now two more recordings had been made – a single featuring 'A Million Songs', written by Joy, with the negro spiritual 'Joshua' on the 'B' side; and an EP (45rpm extended play disc) featuring four songs: 'The Trumpet of the Lord' and 'Walk in the Light', both old Salvation Army songs arranged by Joy, with 'When Jesus Comes to You' written by Joy and 'Yes Indeed!' written by Handel Everett. The group's performance repertoire was building fast.

After some deliberation it was decided that Brenda, Lilian and Thelma should follow the expected course for Salvation Army officer cadets – be ordained, commissioned and given an appointment – and that three more girls who were just finishing the first of their two years in college should be brought into the group as replacements. The guys, Peter and Bill, were also just completing their first year, so it seemed a logical move that the five cadets involved were all in the same year of study. In addition, the string bass player, Captain Handel Everett, a staff member, was also leaving the college and moving on to a new appointment. So personnel changes were needed all around.

Once again Joy made her selection from the girls' choir. She chose Pauline Jane, a top soprano, Ruth Swainsbury, who sang bottom alto, and me, Sylvia Gair, who could sing either soprano or alto. Joy herself could also move easily between soprano and alto, so that vocally it gave the group quite a degree of flexibility.

It cannot have been easy for Brenda, Lilian or Thelma, who had each been involved from the beginning and had soaked up all the excitement of those first months, to quietly accept that they were to move on with their intended vocation. But on reflection we were all extremely disciplined and inclined to go along with the decisions that were made for us. Not one of us three new girls was asked if we wanted to be part of this group, or to take up the responsibilities of public performance and all that it would involve. To each of us it was simply a part of our life of obedience to God and part of our wider ministry in The Salvation Army.

For Pauline, Ruth and me it meant a lot of rehearsal, learning the songs which the others in the group had already sung and recorded, and also lots of new songs that Joy had written. And now the guys, Peter and Bill, were writing too, in order to expand the repertoire and styles still further. It is an amazing thing that up to the time we entered college, none of us had ever written a song. This raises the question – where did all this inspiration for songwriting suddenly come from? We were not just taking hackneyed Church phraseology or even verses of Scripture and setting them to our own music. What we did was to look at the world and the society in which we were living, write lyrics which made people question their own lives, and then set those lyrics to our own contemporary music of the Sixties, which was incredibly varied in style and presentation. Having done that, we prayed that these songs would touch the hearts of those who saw and heard us.

With a six-week summer tour looming, we had to learn how to plan our concerts with a good mix of music. A foot-tapping opening song, full-group vocal songs, dramatic ballads, folk, blue beat (a form of Caribbean ska music), duets, join-in songs, were all interspersed with personal, meaningful testimonies about our Christian faith from group members, until we came to the crux of our concert – the epilogue. During the epilogue, a short but poignant reading from Scripture was presented and relevant comments made by one of the group. Then we would sing one, two or three of our unmistakeable prayer songs. It was during this time that we saw and felt the results of our ministry.

It has been known for this epilogue time to last for anything

Clockwise from top left:
The new line-up (clockwise from left) Pauline, Sylvia, Wycliffe, Ruth, Peter, Bill, Joy; On the summer tour with Lars (next to Joy) and Sandy (Executive Officer, far right); On the summer tour

'What we did was to look at the world and the society in which we were living, write lyrics which made people question their own lives, and then set those lyrics to our own contemporary music of the Sixties'

up to an hour. People would stream forward to stand in front of the stage in acknowledgement of their acceptance of Jesus Christ into their lives. Wherever we presented a concert, the planning committee would have dozens of people ready to counsel those who needed further help in understanding the Christian faith.

1964 SUMMER TOUR

AT the same time as second-year cadets Brenda, Lilian and Thelma were ordained and moved to their respective ministry appointments, the first-year cadets received their summer placements across the country in order to do practical training in ministry. One of the problems for members of the Joystrings, as we were now commonly known, was that apart from Joy and Wycliffe we were still all students expecting summer appointments – but a lot of invitations from various places had come through for the group and had been accepted. The college's solution was that summer placements for Pauline, Ruth, Peter, Bill and me had to be delayed. Instead, we stayed on in residence at the college in order to fulfil these group engagements. In addition, throughout the summer and despite the big commitment to the group, we still had our studies to complete! Captain Sandy Morrice, a staff member of the college, was appointed as our executive officer – or 'liaison manager' as we preferred to call him – and a summer programme of 'performances' was planned with the blessing of the British Commissioner (leader of The Salvation Army in Great Britain), the Training Principal and the General.

For the whole of the summer that year we also had the help of newly ordained Swedish Lieutenant Lars Dunberg whose appointment to Malmö in Sweden was not scheduled until late September, which meant he could play the string bass for the group's engagements.

Looking at that summer programme now, it's as well that at least five of us had an average age of only 20 and all the energy and stamina that goes with that age!

Obviously in order to get to all these venues, we needed something to transport us and all the equipment, which at that time also included a string bass and our personal luggage. The

1964 SUMMER PROGRAMME

May 16-18	Winton Bournemouth (Dorset)
May 19	Cowes (Isle of Wight)
May 20	Shirley, Southampton (Hampshire)
May 21	London (rest day)
May 22	St Paul's Cathedral, London
May 23-24	Bromley (South London)
May 25	11am perform on steps of St Paul's Cathedral (Christian Aid week) evening concert at Balham (London)
May 26	11am perform on steps of St Paul's Cathedral evening concert at Gravesend (Kent)
May 27	11am perform on steps on St Paul's Cathedral evening concert at Nunhead (South London)
May 28	Bexleyheath (South London)
May 29	London (rest day)
May 30	Royal Albert Hall (Annual Methodist Youth Rally)
May 31	Hemel Hempstead (Hertfordshire)
June 1	afternoon concert at the Vauxhall motor factory, Luton (Bedfordshire) evening concert at Luton
June 2	Staines (Surrey)
June 3	High Wycombe (Buckinghamshire)
June 4	Reading (Berkshire)
June 5	London (rest day)
June 6	Northampton Town Hall, Youth for Christ Rally
June 7	Northampton
June 8	Cambridge
June 9	Bedford
June 10	Oxford
June 11	Rushden (Northamptonshire)
June 12	London (rest day)
June 13	Butlin's Holiday Camp, Margate (Kent)
June 14	Margate
June 15-16	Butlin's Holiday Camp, Margate
June 17	Herne Bay (Kent)
June 18	Whitstable (Kent)
June 19	London (rest day)
June 20-21	Felixstowe (Suffolk)
June 22	Stowmarket (Suffolk)
June 23	afternoon Butlin's Holiday Camp, Clacton (Essex) evening concert Clacton Town Hall
June 24	Ipswich (Suffolk)
June 25	Chelmsford (Essex)
June 26	London (rest day)

training college supplied a van for us, but it wasn't quite big enough for seven people and all our equipment. (Wycliffe, our architect drummer, always travelled with his drum kit in his own red sports MG, usually straight from business appointments!)

The only way we could accommodate everything was by having a roof rack on the van, and the big string bass was strapped firmly to this. That was fine, until it rained. Then the string bass had to come inside – usually across our laps – and our suitcases had to go on top of the van instead! The trouble was that in those days the suitcases we had were not waterproof. So on more than one occasion we would arrive at a venue with cases full of wet clothes. The final straw came for us when, after diligently trying to complete college studies while travelling and performing, we arrived at one venue to find our completed hand-written studies ruined by the rain getting inside our cases. Eventually, after a plea to the Principal, we were excused studies whilst on tour!

It is worth interjecting here to tell something more about the Joystrings playing on the steps of St Paul's Cathedral during Christian Aid week. On 26 May 1964 a reporter from *The Daily Telegraph* wrote:

> *The Salvation Army beat group, the Joystrings, hit No 1 spot in town, the steps of St Paul's Cathedral, yesterday. Workmen on the Paternoster building site were almost swinging from their scaffolding, when Pauline Jane and Sylvia Gair, her flaming red hair bursting out of her bonnet, opened with a hot number, 'It's an Open Secret'... The Joystrings have already reached No 26 in the hit parade with this number and certainly the roar of the city traffic was no match for the mighty microphones of the performers, with lunchtime crowds gathering in their hundreds to hear them sing.*

During the three days that we played on the steps of St Paul's, BBC and ITV cameras seemed to be rolling constantly, so that the group was shown repeatedly in the news slots. In addition, articles and photographs appeared in *The Times* and *The Daily Telegraph* newspapers giving the appeal for Christian Aid week good coverage. If Wycliffe couldn't make it to a performance because of his business commitments, it was no problem for Joy to sit down and be at home with a set of drums – as she did on the steps of St Paul's on this occasion – and boy, could she play!

On the first day of June, 1964, prior to giving a concert in Luton, the Joystrings were asked if they would present a short concert to employees at the Luton Vauxhall motor factory during the lunch break. The enthusiasm with which we were received as we played before a crowd of almost 6,000 employees had to be experienced to be believed. Most of those present were not likely to have been churchgoers, but they applauded and called for encores throughout the short concert. I'm not sure that work practice today would allow such a performance to take place on the premises, but we were glad of the opportunity then to be where the people spend the majority of their weekday time.

Many thousands heard the group's message during that summer tour. Newspaper reports state that over the three days at Winton, more than 9,000 people heard the group sing. At Margate during the weekend an estimated 5,000 people were recorded. At Felixstowe, well over 3,000 people were at three different venues throughout the day, and at Butlin's Holiday Camp in Clacton, 2,000 people attended each of the two Joystrings presentations. At Chelmsford, the demand for tickets was so great the venue had to be changed three times before a suitable one large enough was found!

That summer also included recording sessions for radio and television, visits to schools and workers' canteens, meetings with local town dignitaries and countless interviews for local press. In total the six-week summer tour consisted of more than 100 engagements. As an example of a day's schedule: arriving from Cowes on the Isle of Wight on 20 May, we went straight to Central Hall, Southampton, for a sound check, and then on to the Dimplex factory where we gave two one-hour lunchtime concerts to the workers. At 4pm we gave a short concert in Shirley to a crowd of teenagers, and at 5pm we went to TV studios in Southampton for an interview. The day finished with the group giving a concert at Central Hall, followed by a 'spot' in the Park

24

Left: The crowd's view at St Paul's **Above:** Facing the crowds at St Paul's

'Looking at that summer programme now, it's as well that at least five of us had an average age of only 20 and all the energy and stamina that goes with that age!'

Hotel. That totalled six engagements in one day! You could say people got their money's worth. No wonder we needed a rest day after that.

BACK TO STUDIES

AT the end of the summer tour it was time for the five of us who were students to join the programme of the rest of the cadets in our year and take up a summer placement of practical training in ministry, before our second year of in-college study began in October. We each received a placement to Salvation Army corps (churches) close to London so that group rehearsals could still take place, as there were some big engagements to fulfil before we finally returned to full-time college studies.

In fact, we were going to have a new line-up for the start of this new academic year. With Lars Dunberg returning to his appointment in Sweden, Peter now moved from rhythm guitar to bass guitar, with Bill on lead guitar. So now we were seven in the group – four girls and three guys. The only non-singer was Wycliffe our drummer – but Wycliffe could sometimes be heard adding a few 'noises off' from time to time in the more lively, up-beat songs! I should here make mention of the support of Wycliffe's lovely wife, Liz, a schoolteacher. Apart from Wycliffe having to make all kinds of arrangements for his ongoing architectural business while performing with the group, he also had to leave Liz – although she would often turn up at Joystrings events especially when at a London venue. It has to be said that Liz was always one of our most ardent supporters and encouragers.

The next public performance for the group after the summer was on 5–7 September 1964. It was in Scotland, at the annual event known affectionately to Scottish Salvationists as the Scottish Congress. This was, as always, a phenomenal gathering of Christian people for praise and worship and the Joystrings were warmly greeted with thunderous applause. Sadly I missed this event since I had been taken ill with appendicitis a few days earlier, and was instead in a London hospital after undergoing surgery.

However, I was sufficiently recovered to join the group in Cardiff to fulfil engagements for the first weekend in October before we all finally got back to college work. A concert was given in the Cory Hall on Saturday evening and in a cinema on Sunday afternoon, followed by another concert on the Sunday evening. We had clearly been given the directive to get back to college in good time, for the schedule for that evening indicates that we took the 11pm sleeper train from Cardiff, arriving in Paddington, London, very early the following morning!

We continued to attend classes at the college and complete exams, and endeavoured to undertake the other activities our fellow students were involved in, although there were some exceptions. With the permission and blessing of the Training Principal, and in conjunction with the leaders of The Salvation Army in Great Britain, it was felt that we should continue to rehearse, write new songs and make new recordings, as well as accept a *limited* number of performance engagements. As a result, during the autumn term of our second college year we performed in Coventry, played at a reception in London given by

Left: End of year finals for Peter and Bill

the Governor of the Bank of England, went to Wimborne Minster (Bournemouth) to play at an inter-church function, took part in a London City function to aid the Lord Mayor's Christmas Charity Appeal, gave a concert for the children of Barnardo's Homes and played to staff and patients at the Elizabeth Garrett Anderson Hospital (women's hospital) in London for Christmas.

The guidelines for us as cadets, and for Joy as a member of college staff, were to limit our engagements to one weekend and no more than two week-night performances each month. But we had to add to that the rehearsals, plus songwriting and recording time, and so we were soon over-running those guidelines. How this all went down with our fellow cadets, goodness knows, but it was really out of our hands. As they say – 'the show must go on!'

Also during the latter part of 1964 we were rehearsing for a Christmas single written by Joy. This was to prove a huge success for the group, and over the years it has become part of schools' Christmas music. The song, 'A Starry Night', also went straight into the charts. Derric Johnson, world-renowned vocal arranger, and probably best known for the 17 years he served as Creative Consultant for Walt Disney World in Florida, has recently done a beautiful a cappella arrangement of Joy's beautiful song for his vocal orchestration CD *Carol of the Bells* (2008). The flip side of this Joystrings recording was a duo by Peter and Bill, 'Now I Know', a song very much in the close harmony style of Lennon and McCartney.

ORDAINED AND COMMISSIONED

IN January 1965 there were just four months to go to the culmination of life as resident cadets for Peter, Bill, Pauline, Ruth and me. With all this media, music and publicity surrounding us and the group's popularity, we had also to

'Peter now moved from rhythm guitar to bass guitar, with Bill on lead guitar. So now we were seven in the group – four girls and three guys'

work hard to complete study assignments and consider our future as Salvation Army officers.

Ruth was engaged to be married to Lieutenant Cliff Howes as soon as she was ordained in May, so was going to leave the group and begin her life with Cliff. They had received a posting to Treharris in Wales. It was a big adjustment for the group and we all missed Ruth's humour, her companionship and her strong singing voice.

No doubt some heavy deliberations were taking place at the National Headquarters of The Salvation Army, in co-operation with the General, about the future of the Joystrings and how to deal with the appeal of the media and general public to 'hear and see more of them'. In fact, we learned that our days as a group were officially *numbered*. It was thought we would disband in the summer of 1965 following The Salvation Army's great centenary celebrations and our prior ordination as officers. It would seem, though, that after further consultation – and Joy was very much involved in these negotiations – it was decided to let the group continue, without replacing Ruth. But, as I mentioned earlier, the combination of girls' voices we had meant we could all be flexible and so could cover the vocal parts despite her departure.

By that time, untold doors of opportunity for evangelism had opened to the Joystrings and, because of this, for the Church as a whole. Around the country other young people were forming groups styled on the Joystrings and, like us, they were being admitted to venues and events which would otherwise have not been available to the Church. To have disbanded the group after just 18 months I believe would have been a travesty. Thank God, our leaders continued to follow the Holy Spirit's leading in this.

During those final four months of our college days we made many more television appearances, including in January appearing on the *Hallelujah* programme on ABC for 20 minutes.

We also released a new recording, an EP featuring 'Have Faith in God', 'I Want to Sing it', 'Follow' and 'There Was a Man'. There were also concerts in the Eastbrook Hall, Bradford, to 2,500 people; in Leeds Town Hall with 1,800 people; and to 6,000 teenagers over two nights at Westminster Central Hall for the Scripture Union Teenage Rallies under the theme of 'Hitting it Off' (this number included those who had to be accommodated in an overflow hall). At Croydon where we were giving a concert, a crowd of people queued for an hour and a half in cold weather for tickets and, when the hall was full, part of the platform (stage) area was given over to the public in order to seat everyone.

We were also invited to perform in the City of London again, this time in aid of the Feed the Minds campaign on three successive days at the beginning of April. The venues selected for us this time included the Kingsway Hall, former London home of the West London Mission of the Methodist Church, just off Holborn. This hall had become famous for its acoustics and was the home for many recordings of orchestral and film music. It was demolished in 1998 to make way for a hotel of the same name. Our second venue of the week was on the steps of St Paul's Cathedral which was by now very familiar to us. Finally we performed in St Andrew's Church, Holborn Viaduct. In addition, the night before we embarked upon this particular three-day event we were performing at a notable detention centre for hard-core offenders. So much for the guidelines of *limited* performances during our final year of studies!

The enormous understanding of Commissioner Clarence Wiseman, the Training Principal, shown to our extra-mural activities may have been helped by one event held in Regent Hall, Oxford Street, London, in March 1965. This building is still affectionately known to Salvationists as 'The Rink' because it was originally a skating rink. It was bought by The Salvation Army in the 1880s and transformed into a church and outreach centre in the heart of Oxford Street. The Joystrings had been invited to perform on a Saturday night in an upper room of the hall which had been arranged into a club setting. As part of the plan, other students from the training college were to go into the clubs, pubs and coffee bars of Soho with invitations for young people to come to 'God's Night Club' at the hall. Strange as it may seem, the plan worked. The 'club' was packed with young folk ready to listen to the group's music and message. The following day, Sunday, after Commissioner Wiseman's sermon, several young people who had been present the previous evening at the 'club' were among those who accepted Christ for themselves.

It is the custom of The Salvation Army that every new yearly intake of cadets to its officer training college is given a 'sessional' name. Our session was called Proclaimers of the Faith. This proved to be a very significant name indeed, since it encapsulated the whole point of the existence of the Joystrings. Through our music, through our words, in the venues selected for us to play – all our activities centred on proclaiming the Christian faith to which we were all called and committed.

On Friday 14 May 1965, the five of us – Peter, Bill, Pauline, Ruth and I – took our places among 150 cadets of our session at the Royal Albert Hall for our ordination and commissioning as full-time Salvation Army officers. A service of dedication was held in the morning, followed by the ordination and appointments meeting in the afternoon, in which the newly ordained Salvation Army officers heard for the first time the name of the place to which they were being sent, either in sole charge, or alongside a more experienced officer.

Ruth was getting married to Lieutenant Cliff Howes and leaving the group. But for the remainder of the Joystrings members, we were to continue in the group as well as taking

> 'Our session was called Proclaimers of the Faith. It encapsulated the whole point of the existence of the Joystrings'

Top left: Facing the crowds at St Paul's
Above: Meeting the management at the Vauxhall Motor Factory
Far left: Bill catches up on his studies!
Left: Signing autographs at Trafalgar Square

Above: Ruth and Cliff's wedding

Above: Pauline and Keith's wedding

Above: The new lieutenants with General Coutts

Far left: ABC Television presentation
Left: Sylvia and Pauline in duo
Right: Trafalgar Square at the 1965 Centenary Congress

'One of the highlights of the celebrations was the gathering at Trafalgar Square on Saturday 3 July'

flexible placement appointments which would allow us to fulfil group engagements, recordings and whatever else came our way. I was appointed to Holloway, North London, with Captain Vera Gray. She had been an officer on the staff of the college during my first year, so we were not unfamiliar with each other. Pauline went first to New Addington, near Croydon, South London. Within a few weeks she married Lieutenant Keith Banks and then joined him in Enfield, North London. Peter went to Romford in East London, and Bill to Sutton in South London. Since we were all assistants to the senior officers in those corps/churches, I guess the leaders thought we could be free to fulfil our Joystrings duties quite easily.

However, settling into placements which were to be part-time was not easy for any of the group members. We had lost our student base, the college. Now, when we needed to rehearse or meet for engagements we had to come from different parts of London. This meant our travelling times were much longer and more complex. Getting back 'home' following a late concert also presented problems. Until Bill got his driving licence, Peter was the only driver of the van, so he was always the last to arrive home – usually in the early hours of the morning. Years later, when Peter and I came back to live in London following our marriage, he was always glad he had learned well how to drive the back streets of London in record time! However, being the young fledgling lieutenants that we were, we took the difficulties in our stride and continued to rack up the hours in songwriting, rehearsals and performances, and in between all this endeavoured to do some practical parish work in our respective London areas.

INTERNATIONAL CENTENARY CELEBRATIONS

SALVATIONISTS will be aware that 1965 marked the centenary of the birth of The Salvation Army, and of course all kinds of special events had been planned as part of those celebrations. The music and rhythm of the Joystrings was naturally going to be included in these celebrations, so that much of our time was taken up with rehearsals and briefing for these special events.

On Friday 25 June, for instance, we were back at the Royal Albert Hall for The Festival of Youth, along with brass bands from Canada and Sweden, Australian timbrelists and groups from Scotland, Ireland and Wales.

From all over the world had come thousands of international Salvationist delegates and performing groups, young and old, uniformed and non-uniformed. On one day they gathered in the grounds of Crystal Palace, perhaps better known for its football club down the road. Nevertheless the venue was perfect on Saturday 26 June, a glorious sunny day, for a field day to surpass all other London field days, with 50,000 people gathered for marches, parades, music, games and youth activities taking place. The sound of this monumental gathering rolled out across South London in a salute to the past and a promise for the future. For the Joystrings on that day, signing autographs was all part of the job!

Tuesday 29 June saw us performing twice. In the afternoon we were at the Westminster Central Hall for the Women's Rally, and in the evening in the same venue for the Centenary Youth Rally. The following day we were back at the Royal Albert Hall in the afternoon for the Seniors Rally! I guess we must have been covering all the age groups.

One of the highlights of the celebrations was the gathering at Trafalgar Square on Saturday 3 July. We set up our equipment on the plinth at the bottom of Nelson's Column, between the lions, and played to the crowds from there. From that vantage point we could be seen and heard and we could also see across the sea of faces gathered in one of London's most famous tourist spots.

We had made successful appearances at Barkers Departmental Store in Kensington, and then Selfridges of Oxford Street also invited us to play in their store. There, on the third floor, on a specially erected platform, we played to hundreds of people who had crowded in to hear us. Feet tapped, hands clapped and people were moved with emotion when it came to the presentation of our quiet message-filled songs. In contrast, within days of that appearance we were playing to hordes of youngsters at Olympia at The *Daily Mail* Schoolboys and Schoolgirls Exhibition. What wonderful opportunities of ministry!

Above: In rehearsal at the training college

Above: Uniform changes

CHANGES

THE JOYSTRINGS

WITH SO MANY INVITATIONS TO appear on television, the complexities of lighting and quick changes of instrumentation for some members of the group became important matters. TV producers and floor managers were beginning to suggest the possibility of some minor changes to our uniform. Remember that for our programmes then, nothing was ever pre-recorded. All our television presentations were live – what you saw was what you got, mistakes as well!

The suggestion was made that we had a grey uniform instead of the dark navy, and that a much lighter material would be more suitable because working under studio lighting for hours could become very hot. And perhaps the girls could remove their traditional bonnets too? That would certainly make it easier and quicker for Joy when she switched from guitar to keyboard and back again. Now, we didn't have authority to make those changes, even for TV, without the permission of our Salvation Army leaders. Grey uniforms were certainly being worn by officers who worked in warm climates like Africa and India, and were not unknown in the UK either. So no one objected to that. As for the bonnets? – well, we had clearly established that we were a Salvation Army group, our identity was known worldwide by now, and if it made the whole business of studio and concert performance work more 'comfortable' for us and easier for TV crews working with us, then so be it. Permission was granted to leave off the bonnets.

Needless to say, when the girls first dispensed with their bonnets for performances, letters followed from some Salvationists who thought we were traitors to the cause. 'I feel ashamed of you,' wrote one songster (member of an adult choir in a corps), and 'They should be made to conform to the rules,' wrote another. We hope that by now those Salvationists have forgiven us for doing what we thought best enhanced the way we presented the gospel in these new God-given opportunities.

But you know what? All our performances were invariably in full official uniform, no matter what the event, venue or temperature, and our uniforms served to make us instantly recognisable as part of The Salvation Army we represented!

By the end of the summer of 1965 the leaders of The Salvation Army realised that having the members of the group situated and working from different places in London and the suburbs just wasn't working, either for the corps involved or for us. So it was decided to bring Peter, Bill and me to work alongside Joy at National Headquarters in Queen Victoria Street in the City of London. Joy had by then been appointed to the Music Department, then under the leadership of Major Brindley Boon and under whose umbrella the Joystrings tours and events took place.

Following their marriage in the summer, Pauline and Keith were living and working at Enfield, North London, so Pauline could easily continue her Joystrings work with Keith's blessing. Now we were operating under the direction of the Army's National HQ Music Department and had a room in 101 Queen Victoria Street where we could rehearse together regularly. It made things so much easier and tidier!

With invitations flooding in, someone decided we needed a new touring vehicle with the group's name clearly defined on each side of the van. This proved to be a great deterrent against Peter and Bill speeding up and down the motorways, and of course it always drew hoots and waves from passing motorists. Whenever we arrived in a town or city, bystanders were left in no doubt at all as to who was being transported and this clearly advertised our arrival!

A tour of Manchester followed soon after we took possession of the new vehicle, and soon afterwards a visit to Guildford Cathedral for yet another Centenary Service of Thanksgiving. Later it was back to London for our second stint at performing for the Feed the Minds campaign. This time we were presenting our music from the deck of the Thames launch *MS Abercorn*, moored on the Embankment

> 'Letters followed from some Salvationists who thought we were traitors to the cause...'

Above: On tour in the new van **Right:** A little help from our friends **Below:** On board *HMS Victorious*

at Westminster. Making the introductions and leading carols that night was Sonia Rees, who was then playing the role of Maria in *The Sound of Music* at the Palace Theatre.

By November we were ready with a new EP recording, *Christmas with The Joystrings* featuring 'This Little Boy', 'What Dreams', 'Such a Tiny Child' and 'Winter's Coming On'. ABC Television gave the group 45 minutes on Christmas Day to promote the new recording and present other Christmas songs. Sadly, this was the last recording Pauline was to make with us. Shortly after her marriage she became seriously ill, and although she bravely continued to sing with the Joystrings for a further six months, her failing health forced her eventually to withdraw from the hectic and constant round of engagements. Of course we had to accept and respect her decision, but we would miss her beautiful soprano voice. Once again the group was facing a transition time and a readjustment in the vocal line up.

We finished the year by touring the Black Country, performing at Hanley, Cannock and Macclesfield. One young girl had sold over a hundred tickets to her school friends for the performance in the Victoria Hall, Hanley. Needless to say, with such enthusiasm they managed to fill the front rows.

ON THE ROAD

AS 1965 gave way to 1966 so the five of us who remained – Joy, Peter, Bill, Wycliffe and I – settled into a cycle of travelling, giving concerts, writing songs, recording, and television and radio presentations. At the beginning of the year we were in Hadleigh, Essex, in the Kingsway Theatre playing to 1,400 people. Many more were disappointed because the tickets had sold out. It was the same in Carlisle in the Market Hall with 1,600 in the audience on Saturday evening. And on Sunday more than 1,000 people came back for the afternoon and evening worship services held in the same venue.

If singing in a departmental store was thought to be unusual, then surely the invitation for us to perform from the deck of the aircraft carrier *HMS Victorious* which was docked in Southampton, during our visit to Portsmouth, was even more so.

We gave a concert in Portsmouth Guildhall to more than 2,000 people on the Saturday evening and presented our music from the aircraft carrier on Sunday afternoon.

Following a second programme given by the Joystrings on ABC's *Hallelujah* series on TV, we received second place in the ratings for the most popular religious programme in January with 3.45 million viewers, beaten – only just! – by *Songs of Praise* with 3.50 million.

It was a first for us when we visited Southall Grammar School early in 1966. In the afternoon lessons were suspended so that all 700 pupils could attend the concert we were presenting in the school assembly hall. A few days later we were at the Ealing Grammar School to repeat the whole process. Over the five years of our existence we visited many schools and we were more than happy to be able to present our music and message to the young folk.

Macclesfield, Derby, Ripley, Bedford, Northampton, Nottingham, Boston and Kettering were all on our engagement list for the first part of 1966. But remember, it wasn't just for an evening concert. Being on the road was hard work. We did not have 'roadies' to unpack, set up or dismantle our equipment – we did it all ourselves. Peter, Bill and Wycliffe had a special way of fitting the equipment into the van so that it fitted snugly and didn't encroach on the seating area for the group members. Joy and I were in charge of wrapping up cables and microphones and seeing to all the 'lighter' stuff. So after a late concert – which always included speaking with fans, signing autographs and so on – we'd pack up the van and often try to move on to our next venue that same night, sometimes arriving at our overnight accommodation well after midnight.

Accommodation for us in those days did not mean hotels. It was normal practice for us instead to stay with kindly Salvationists or church people who generously opened their homes to us at some ungodly hour. It was not unusual, feeling absolutely dead tired, for us to have to sit down with our hosts to a supper they had lovingly prepared hours earlier and try to be 'sparkling' with conversation. In fact, what we each really needed was just to crawl into bed and not be at all sociable. However, we are still enormously grateful for the kindness and understanding shown

Above: After the show is over

us from all those who hosted us over that five-year period!
The next morning it was often off to the town hall for a mayoral reception given on behalf of the town we were visiting, and then perhaps a workers' canteen lunchtime concert or a visit a school, and then on to prepare for the evening concert. After which we would start the whole process over again…

So perhaps it wasn't surprising when, after weeks of travelling and living like this, Bill collapsed from sheer exhaustion while was singing one of his solos on the last night of this particular tour at Peterborough. Thankfully, after taking a rest period he was fine again. But it was a warning to us all, and to those who were planning our tours and events, to be more careful.

We couldn't have been allowed much rest though, as by Easter we were up in Scotland, in Aberdeen's Music Hall, playing to a capacity crowd of more than 2,000 people. After the interval in that concert, Bill and Peter returned to the stage wearing kilts and were piped in by a piper of the city police pipe band in full Highland dress. You can imagine the tumultuous applause this caused.

4

JOYSTRINGS
ABROAD

FRANCE

AFTER travelling on the overnight sleeper train from London, we arrived at the Gare du Nord in Paris early one morning in April 1966 and unloaded our equipment into the back of the waiting van belonging to the Salvation Army headquarters there. Captain Jill Buchanan, an English officer and personal friend of Joy's, met us and was our interpreter for the weekend. After breakfast we were given a whistle-stop tour of Paris, ending up at the Salvation Army training college for officers where we sang to the students there. Following lunch we were whisked off to the Paris TV studios where we rehearsed some songs for the *Tour de Monde* show which was transmitted live at 7pm the next day. Thankfully we had rehearsed singing Bill's song 'Lord on our Side' in French – at least the chorus.

This brief encounter with Paris was just a taster. The following month we were to return to take part in a rally for young people conducted by the second in command of the international Salvation Army, the Chief of the Staff, Commissioner Erik Wickberg. However, before this and within hours of arriving back in England we were travelling again, this time to play to the boys at Hollesley Bay Borstal institution near Woodbridge in Suffolk. The resident boys there had helped a great deal in the building of the chapel where we played. And then it was on to Durham, Darlington, Middlesbrough and Guisborough, where the people of the north took us to their hearts and turned out in their thousands to hear us. We certainly had to be flexible in our approach to very mixed audiences, from the north to the south of the country, to the churched and the un-churched, to those in prison and out of prison, and most of the time we were relying on strength other than our own and certainly on a guiding hand over all our endeavours.

THE NETHERLANDS

BEFORE returning to Paris we were invited to appear on Dutch television. The programme was recorded in the large theatre of NCRV studios in Hilversum before an audience of 2,000 young people on 2 May and was to be shown on 8 May when we would be in Paris. Here we also had the chance to perform alongside the legendary American gospel singer Marion Williams.

In between all of our touring and concerts, we had also been working on yet another recording with EMI, knowing that we needed to produce something different for our continental visits. The EP *Joystrings Abroad* was released just before we left for the Netherlands, with two of the songs – 'Lord on our Side' and 'Time' – partly in French. The flip side 'Love That's in My Heart' and 'Without Him' were both in English.

RETURN TO PARIS

THIS time we took a plane to Paris and went straight to the youth rally on Saturday afternoon in a crowded Paris Central Hall. Even a power failure halfway through the concert did not daunt the enthusiasm of the Paris youth. They stomped, clapped and shouted, and when the power returned, joined very loudly with the singing.

At the Top Ten Club, now called Club 79, which is located at 79 Ave des Champs-Élysées, we played between 9pm and 2am (that's right, two in the morning!). This was one of our toughest ever assignments. We had no French language ourselves apart from the two songs we had recorded, and the music in the club by the other bands who were on the show was at a volume that was simply unbelievable, even to us! None of us was ever sure any message we were trying to give reached the hearts or ears of anyone present. We did not feel comfortable or convinced about this venue, yet the Salvation Army leaders of France believed, in good faith, that this was one place we should be seen and heard.

The next day, despite getting to our beds at about 3am, we left at 9.30am to travel to the Morfondé boys' home in the north-eastern suburbs of Paris. This centre was then a Salvation Army training farm for teenage boys in need of correctional services. We were amazed at what these boys were learning. Besides acquiring skills in farming, they also had a workshop where they were creating beautiful pieces of jewellery in metalcraft with enamelling. I still have the piece I was given there and I treasure it because of the memory connected with it. I wore it proudly for years and it really went with the Sixties fashion. After a guided tour of the training centre, we gave a short concert for the boys and this was filmed by a French television company.

It is interesting to see that after all these years Morfondé is still a Salvation Army training centre for young people. It offers protection, education, training and integration for a wide range of young people aged from 12 to 25 years of age, some of whom are referred through the courts or the child welfare system. Its aim is to stabilise youth behaviour problems. Alternating between theory and practice in small groups, these youngsters are encouraged to build self-esteem, connect with society and learn a trade or pursue an education which will equip them for their future life. So the work continues in the Morfondé Professional Education Centre, and it has always held a special place in the hearts of the Joystrings.

We arrived mid-afternoon at the *Lycée Carnot* in Paris. This was a school where once again we played to the children for a short time before moving on to Montmartre to set up our equipment in the large Salvation Army centre there. However, just before our performance in the evening gathering, which did not commence until 8.30pm, the French organisers were determined to get their 'pound of flesh' by having us perform *outside*, on a concourse in Montmartre, using only acoustic guitars. Perhaps the idea was to draw even more people into the evening event. But we soon discovered that these were proving to be long days

'The Salvation Army leaders of France believed that this was one place we should be seen and heard'

and nights and we were running low on adrenalin on what was only our second day in France.

The next day, Friday 6 May, was a little more relaxed, with just a morning reception with Paris dignitaries at the *Hôtel de Ville* followed by a short presentation of music outside, during which members of the press could take photographs. Then we moved on to the YMCA of Paris, where we were entertained to lunch. This was followed by a free afternoon when we could see something more of the city, before doing another publicity photo shoot in the evening at the *Palais de la Femme*, The Salvation Army's hostel for more than 600 women students, at 94, Rue de Charonne.

On Saturday over 1,000 people gathered in the cavernous restaurant of the *Palais de la Femme* to hear us sing again. In the evening the Paris Central

Left: Outside the Top Ten club, Paris
Above: Performing in the Top Ten Club

Hall was absolutely packed with young people for the Festival of Youth in which we sang and spoke. On that day, many of those French young people responded to a call to commitment. Sunday was a devotional day for all those young people who had met for special services, and our French tour concluded on Monday morning when we revisited the students of the Salvation Army college for officer training.

From Paris we hastened back to London where we were scheduled to play once again on behalf of Christian Aid week on the steps of St Paul's Cathedral from 16-21 May during the lunch break.

It was a great privilege to be invited by the organisers of events celebrating the 900th anniversary of Westminster Abbey, to take part in a special service there for young people on 4 June 1966. We sang three songs appropriate to the solemnity and theme of the occasion, which celebrated the lives of young people: 'There will be God', 'Without Him' and 'One Life to Live'. Reflecting on that occasion now, I find it hard to believe that all those years ago, aged just 21, I was honoured to sing my own song 'Without Him' in that great church!

Below left: In full swing at the Top Ten Club
Below right: Ready to begin the performance
Top right: Victory march along the Champs-Élysées following the performance!

Left: Playing outside the *Hôtel de Ville*, Paris

45

ALL
YOU NEED
IS LOVE

JUST SO THAT WE DIDN'T FORGET WHAT we were all about, it wasn't long before we set off on our travels once again, this time headed for South Wales, where we played in Senghenydd, Cardiff and Newport.

In fact Newport was to be my last public performance with the group for a while. Over the course of the previous year Peter and I realised our personal relationship was much more than friendship. In June 1966 we announced our engagement. Because being in the group together was so public and being on the road all the time a tremendous strain, Peter and I decided after some thought that it would be better if I took a break for a few months to give our relationship some space. After all, the way things had gone over the past three years, we were never out of each other's company. So I was appointed to New Addington, near Croydon, the place where Pauline had her summer placement for a few weeks. I knew it would be hard for me to be away, for I loved singing and loved the work the group was doing. But the other group members understood that I had to go ahead with this short break.

Sadly for me, I was to miss the group's presentation, with Sir Bernard Miles and some actor friends at the Mermaid Theatre on the Thames Embankment in July, of *The Gift of Tongues*. This was a programme of readings from the Bible and Christian poets, often in humorous forms of dialect from around the country. The music of the Joystrings bound the programme together and included music by the children of Great Sampford Primary School in Essex. On that occasion Peter's sister, Christine, stood in for me, singing my vocal parts.

THE WARMONGERS

THE thought that I was to give myself a break from media attention for a few months was short-lived – and here the story temporarily becomes my personal episode. Within weeks I was approached by Major Will Pratt, International Public Relations Secretary for The Salvation Army at the time, who asked me to take a lead role in a musical documentary about The Salvation Army's evangelistic and social work. Granada Television Company had been planning this for some time and had already approached a London West End actor, Gerard Hely, to take the other lead role. It would seem I had become 'available' at exactly the right time.

After initial discussions about the documentary and my role, I was not at all sure that I was the right person. After all, I was going to have to present, both in song and spoken word, what The Salvation Army believed in, our mission mandate, the reasons behind our social work and other important issues. I was 22 years old, a newly commissioned officer and, in my mind, totally inadequate for this task! In contrast, Gerard was a seasoned actor, almost twice my age, and his role was to put across his own atheistic point of view during the documentary. He was to challenge me strongly when I talked about my personal Christian faith, and how The Salvation Army functions as a Christian organisation and still manages to attract and hold the loyalty of so many people in this day and age.

Despite my fears, I was assured by Will Pratt that I was the right person to do it. My already widely known profile on television and with the media gave me an immediate link with viewers and would just be an extension of what I had done recently with the Joystrings, he said confidently. So with the blessing of the officer in charge of New Addington, Captain Joyce Dixon, with whom I was working, I embarked on filming *The Warmongers*. Lasting 45 minutes, this was to be the first in a series of *This England* programmes.

It took many weeks, flying between London and Manchester almost weekly, to film various sections of the programme – our work among the homeless and alcoholics and with the fractured families that the Army was engaged in helping with furniture, clothing and food. We also filmed services in the 'church' part of the Army, and Gerard and I discussed for hours aspects of faith and doctrine, only some of which was used for the documentary.

However, it was a musical documentary and, strange as it may seem, we had to learn music written for the programme by British composer Arthur Butterworth, better known for his symphonies, concertos, orchestral scores, chamber music and his not inconsiderable amount of 'serious' music for brass. The lyrics presented questions and answers in a pseudo-operatic style. Gerard was much more comfortable with this genre than I was. The rest of the musical backdrop to this intriguing programme was recorded in one intensive day's work at the Granada studios. The complicated scoring by Butterworth was handled well by Stockport Citadel Band under the leadership of Colin Wilson and Manchester Openshaw Songsters under Harry Salthouse. Major Brindley Boon, under whose managership the Joystrings were then working, was responsible that day for seeing everything ran smoothly as far as the musical sections were concerned. Ironically, the person who was to replace me during my break from the group, Nigel Robson, was also to be seen, albeit momentarily, as he appeared in the documentary playing his guitar with a local group from Stockport which provided some of the backing music.

There was one humorous moment I should mention that occurred during the many days of filming. I was set up on a soap-box, outside Manchester's old Star Hall (one of The Salvation Army's corps buildings, now demolished) to hold an impromptu solo open-air meeting. A crowd had been gathered from nearby flats to provide the necessary listeners for my 'preaching'. It wasn't difficult to draw in a large crowd – after all, there were lots of television cameras and crew around. The idea was that Gerard, placed strategically in the midst of the assembled crowd, would begin to heckle me and I had to defend myself with appropriate words. However, Gerard was totally unprepared for the wave of public sympathy which went out to me when he dared to challenge this young Army lass doing her best, on her own, in such a tough area of Manchester. One or two stout-hearted listeners, who had probably never seen the inside of a Salvation Army building, were more than prepared to do battle against Gerard on my behalf! In fact, I think at one point Gerard had to make a quick get-away as one dear soul raised her umbrella and took more than a step towards him. These people took it to be a genuine attack on me and my Christian beliefs. I am not sure the producer, Peter Plummer, ever got what he really wanted from that section of the filming. The programme was aired on 8 March 1967 at 9.45pm and eventually was nominated

Above: Joy with Sir Bernard Miles **Below:** *The Warmongers* in the *TV Times* television listings

for an award at the Monte Carlo Television Festival for 'best documentary'. Without the recent experience of my work with the Joystrings, the years of media exposure and handling the press, I could never have done this.

With me taking a break from the group for a few months it meant that once again the group vocals and line-up had to go through a transition.

NIGEL

BILL knew of a young and very talented musician from Stockport in Manchester, who had recently left school and was available! The son of Salvation Army officers, Nigel Robson came from a gifted family and had already established himself as a brilliant lead guitarist in a local Salvation Army group called The Persuaders. In addition he was a keyboard player and had a great tenor voice. After a few rehearsals it certainly looked and sounded as if Nigel would slot into the group quite easily and add a new dimension. A much heavier rock sound emerged during the time that he was part of the Joystrings, and evidence of the change in composition and sound can be heard on the Christmas LP *Well Seasoned*, recorded in the autumn of 1966 and featuring some of Nigel's arrangements.

It must have been tough on Nigel, coming right into the middle of a busy Joystrings schedule. He had to pick up on the whole repertoire, catch up almost three years of the group's history and appear as if he was 'born to it'. This was also his first time living away from home and the family he loved dearly. Now he had to learn to adjust to living in London, and at the same time throw himself into this new arena of being a real 'pop' star. He joined the Editorial Department staff at The Salvation Army's headquarters in London as his 'base' job. He had written three years earlier about his discovery of Bach and the impact this composer had on his life. So when I returned to the group a couple of months before my marriage to Peter in July 1967, Nigel was considering pursuing his real love – classical music.

The autumn programme of 1966 took the group to Winchester Guildhall, where it was filled to capacity twice in one day;

The young sing for the aged in London

The Salvation Army Joy Strings singing on the steps of St. Paul's Cathedral last week

and to Broadway Baptist Church in Chesham, with more than 1,000 people present, the largest congregation any church had seen in Chesham in many years. From there it was on to Nottingham and then up to Glasgow, where a lunchtime show in Lewis's department store in Argyle Street was scheduled. This was followed by a performance for the pupils of Bellahouston Academy, where the group was treated to a screaming welcome usually reserved for the Beatles or the Rolling Stones. A concert at St Mungo's Hall completed the autumn tour.

In October in Southend the group gave a concert to shoppers in Keddies department store (this store closed in the mid-nineties), before an evening performance at the Cliffs Pavilion. It was then on to Butlin's Holiday Camp at Clacton and the Gaiety Theatre, where the group's performance brought The Salvation Army's holiday week to a moving conclusion.

Torquay, Plymouth, Redruth, Exeter and Salisbury all received the Joystrings during that season with warm enthusiasm. Norwich, Sheringham and Yarmouth were next on the schedule, when – horror of horrors! – for the first time in three years Joy was ill with flu and simply couldn't make this particular tour. I was called back to sing Joy's vocal parts. Fortunately, I had only been four months out, so there were no drastic changes. With 1,500 people present at the Yarmouth Hippodrome, the group's

Above: Nigel steps in **Right:** *The Warmongers* in the *TV Times* **Far right:** The photograph of Sylvia used in media promotion for *The Warmongers*

performance was a far cry from the usual circus acts which perform in the 'ring' in the summer season.

And although Wycliffe was present for the Norwich performance, business commitments did not allow him to go on to Sheringham the following day. So a drummer was borrowed from the Salvation Army corps at Norwich Citadel. Roger Woodrow proved himself to be a very able pop drummer, so much so that on other occasions afterwards, when Wycliffe couldn't make a performance, Roger was often ready to step into his shoes!

In November 1966 the Joystrings were invited to Liverpool. Peter, Bill and Wycliffe had all spent some of their youth in that city, so it was a memorable visit for them. But it was also special for all the group members, since there was an invitation to play in the world-famous Cavern Club, where the Beatles famously did some of their inaugural work. The Joystrings were scheduled to perform at midnight and were introduced to the hundreds of young people who had crowded into the club as 'a group with

a difference'. In the two hours the Joystrings were in the Cavern they sang and spoke of the reason for 'the difference' in their lives and music. This was their second midnight concert in a row, as the previous night they had played at midnight at one of Shell's sports clubs en route from Cefn Mawr, North Wales, where they had given a concert.

In fact this short tour to North Wales and Liverpool took the group to youth clubs, sports clubs, a motor factory, a grammar school, a church and finally to Liverpool's Philharmonic Hall, where they gave a concert to 2,000 people gathered there. The group must have made quite an impression on the people of Liverpool, because just a few weeks later they were back to Liverpool Cathedral to take part in a special Christmas service for the young people of the city.

JOYSTRINGS

mono

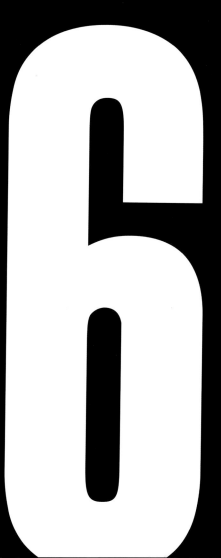

6

THE JOYSTRINGS

AS YOU CAN IMAGINE, THE LEAD up to Christmas always brought a wide gamut of invitations. Tom Jones, whose 'Green, Green Grass of Home' was Number 7 in the charts at the time, invited the Joystrings to be on his 45-minute *Tom Jones Christmas Radio Show* to be transmitted on Christmas afternoon. The show was well documented at the time in *The Musical Express*.

Cliff Richard showed great interest in the Joystrings, since he had become a Christian in 1964 and had become involved in presenting Christian gospel shows. He invited the group to support him on one of his gospel tours of Spain and Portugal, the request being submitted to The Salvation Army's leaders in London. However, the request was turned down. The reason given was that there was no Salvation Army (at that time) in either of those countries, and that therefore the tour would be on a completely different footing from anything else the group had previously undertaken.

The decision was perhaps surprising, since up to that time Salvation Army leadership had been so liberal in wanting the Joystrings to go to places where The Salvation Army normally didn't get a look in. Spain and Portugal would have been virgin ground! However, Cliff didn't give up altogether and didn't seem to hold the decision against the group personally. He had quite a discussion with Bill about the new Joystrings LP released for Christmas 1966, *Well Seasoned*. In fact, a short time after the Joystrings as a group had ended, Joy was invited to a charity event with Cliff and the two of them were photographed together. Not for the first time has it been thought that Joy and Cliff were brother and sister (Cliff's birth name being Harry Webb)! Time after time Joy has assured people that they are in no way related.

Around the same time, the *Daily Mail* and *Daily Mirror*

> 'Cliff Richard showed great interest in the Joystrings, since he had become a Christian in 1964 and had become involved in presenting Christian gospel shows'

announced that ITV's popular *Hippodrome* variety show, which had a kind of circus format, would feature the Joystrings alongside actor and American country music singer Jimmy Dean and actress Anita Gillette. The show also included timbrelists from Hendon Salvation Army who gave a scintillating display of dexterity – plus two lions, three tigers, four leopards, a black panther and a puma which were also on the guest list as part of the earlier circus act. I wonder what the Founder of The Salvation Army, William Booth, would have made of all this? Certainly it is recorded that he made good use of circus tents.

Selfridges department store in London's Oxford Street invited the group to perform for four days to their customers in the days before Christmas, and the producers of the radio programme *Home This Afternoon*, a programme for older listeners, also featured the Joystrings, together with The Salvation Army's International Staff Band, on air just before Christmas.

And that was not all. There was also a hospital performance; two appearances at the Fairfield Halls, Croydon; *Christmas with The Salvation Army* at Westminster Central Hall; playing on St Paul's Cathedral steps again for the Help the Aged Appeal; and playing in Trafalgar Square for the switch-on of the Christmas tree lights – these were all on the December schedule for the group. Perhaps worth more than just a mention is the Christmas Benefit Concert in aid of the Aberfan Disaster Fund at the Royal Albert Hall, where the Joystrings featured alongside the Small Faces and Cat Stevens. It is interesting to note that at the time of the Aberfan disaster, former Joystrings member Ruth and her husband Cliff Howes were the Salvation Army officers in the South Wales valley and selflessly served the people there in the aftermath of that great tragedy.

Top left: Hendon Timbrellists join the Joystrings on the *Hippodrome* show
Above: On the rooftops of London with Nigel
Left: Tom Jones chats with Bill after the show
Far left: Joy with Cliff Richard

In addition the group appeared on Swedish television in a programme showing unusual musical presentations used in church enterprise. The Joystrings were featured in extracts from the film *Tragedies of Affluence* for which they provided background music. The film was an offshoot from a special report by The Salvation Army to mark its centenary in 1965 and highlighted the Army's work among marginalised people in Britain. Also in December, French television transmitted shots of the group performing at the carol service in the Fairfield Halls, Croydon.

This incredible high-profile exposure in a professional world may be thought to have been alien to the Joystrings. But it just continued to snowball and astound everyone, confirming the feelings of all involved that this work was indeed of the Holy Spirit. This, beyond all doubt, was God's perfect timing for the Christian gospel to be right in the midst of the world of popular music and presentation.

SONG BREAK

THE new year 1967 set off at a tremendous pace for the Joystrings when the regional TV company ABC Television invited the group to take part in *Song Break*. This was intended to be a short series of programmes filmed and recorded in workplaces around the country, either in the canteen or on the factory floor of large industrial firms in the Midlands and North of England. The factory's own choir and employees were always featured, and John Lawrenson was the resident tenor soloist and compère. Transmitted weekly at 6.35pm on Sunday evenings, the series, which began broadcasting on 19 February, drew in up to 2.5 million viewers – more than the national BBC's *Songs*

RELIGION

The Joystrings take their brand of music into a church service on Sunday — JOAN ELLIOTT reporting

The Joystrings . . . "an exciting occasion for us", says group leader Captain Joy Webb

POP IN THE EYES OF THE LORD

IT was probably the American negroes who first translated their Christian faith into folk music. It seemed normal to them in the days of their slavery to sing their love of the Lord, and since then the Negro Spiritual has had an honoured place in music of the people.

It is surprising then to realise the birth of the Joystrings, the Salvation Army's pop group, should have aroused any controversy. Tambourines the public were used to, but guitars and

The drummer in the group

The new Silksworth Independent Methodist Church

Above: *The Viewer* reports the visit to New Silksworth **Right:** Recording for *Song Break*

of Praise at the time. It proved so popular that it was extended for 18 weeks until 18 June. The programme was designed to show the relevance of Christian faith to everyday living, and it was a testament to the Joystrings that the programme's producers considered the group's aim and function to be precisely that.

Never before or since, in Britain, has a Salvation Army group received such lengthy continuous presentation on television. Here again was a God-given opportunity for communicating the Christian gospel to a huge TV audience.

Another great opportunity came when the group was invited by Charles Grey, Labour Member of Parliament for Durham and a Methodist minister, to conduct a full 60-minute service for Tyne Tees Television. This was televised live from the New Silksworth Independent Methodist Church, County Durham, on Sunday 9 April and broadcast throughout the whole ITV network. This was the first time the Joystrings had been seen on TV conducting a full worship service as distinct from performing music alone. It was perhaps a mark of how respected the group's work had become in the world of broadcasting. In this production the Joystrings chose part of *The Folk Gospel*, a narrative of biblical, classical and poetry readings put together by Wycliffe with specially written music, which traced the gospel story from the beginning through to the modern day and demonstrated its relevance to mankind.

While the Joystrings were in the northeast of the country, the group was given an opportunity to record a series of seven epilogues for Tyne Tees TV. Then in February the BBC's *Songs of Praise* broadcast from Peterborough Salvation Army Citadel also featured the Joystrings.

Above: All aboard! Sylvia's back

7

SCANDINAVIAN
TOUR

THE JOYSTRINGS

IT WAS UNDERSTOOD THAT I WAS going to return to the group some time before my marriage to Peter which was planned for 8 July 1967. That being so, Joy thought it best to bring me back in for all rehearsals, recordings and publicity shoots for the group's proposed Scandinavian tour at the end of April. Nigel, who had made a very special contribution during his short stay as a member of the group, was returning to study and moving on to classical music. He has since made a distinguished career in this field as a lyric tenor and become a star in his own right, and his appearances are still sought after.

The London Transport Museum in Clapham was selected as one of the locations for a new photo shoot. Since London was our base, what better than a London bus as a background for a good picture? The museum is full of interesting locomotives, trams and buses, and I think Peter and Bill almost forgot the reason they were there – as did a group of schoolchildren on an educational outing with a teacher at the same time. When they caught sight of our Joystrings' uniforms, Queen Adelaide's train-coach with the gold-plated door handles and Mr Shillibeer's horse omni-bus ('a shilling for any journey') were quite forgotten, as they rushed towards us with pieces of paper and pens at the ready for autographs!

Since the Scandinavian tour would take us away for over two weeks without a break, Wycliffe did not feel he could leave his architect's practice for such an extended period of time. So once again Roger, from Norwich, came along for good measure and played the drums when Wycliffe wasn't able to be there.

It was also decided to take photographs of the group in front of the Houses of Parliament with Joy and me in Norwegian costume. It seems that even the London policemen wondered what was happening on their beat that day. These costumed photographs were used on the special production Scandinavian version of a new EMI EP recording we had cut especially for this tour under the title of *The Song Break*. It featured the songs 'Tomorrow', 'Everything', 'This is Living' and 'It Won't Always Be like This'. The UK version of the EP had one of the London Transport Museum photos on its sleeve.

SWEDEN

WE sailed from Harwich to Copenhagen with our van full of equipment on board. On arrival at Copenhagen we transferred to the *MS Öresund* passenger ferry which would take us to Malmö in Sweden. Can you believe that after all that travelling, when we eventually arrived in Sweden at 9.30pm, we had to have a preliminary meeting with a TV producer – because immediately following breakfast the next morning we were to record for Swedish TV? That same evening, having spent the morning in the TV studios, we gave a concert beginning at 8pm in The Admiral Dance Hall in the city. This was typical of our touring schedule.

The following day, Saturday, we travelled almost 200 miles to Jönköping, where we gave two concerts, one at 7pm and the next beginning at 10pm, both in the Salvation Army worship hall. They had to have two concerts since they had sold enough tickets to fill the hall twice! This raises the question, wasn't there a bigger venue in Jönköping at the time?

The next day was Sunday and thankfully we had only 25 miles to travel to Tranås where we met for a worship service with fellow Salvationists. Then we drove another 25 miles, this time to Motala where, on the city centre flag poles, a Union Jack and a Salvation Army flag were flown in our honour. We gave an afternoon concert in the Salvation Army worship centre, leaving afterwards to drive just over 40 miles to Norrköping where at 8pm we gave a concert in Norrköping Sports Hall.

Thank goodness, the following day was scheduled as a free day – apart from the fact that we had to drive 110 miles to Stockholm. But after dinner we were able to explore the city. Our hosts were kind enough to allow the next morning for shopping or just to relax, before we set up our equipment in the Folkets Hus Congress Hall, an impressive city conference centre built in 1960 with the main auditorium seating 1,400. Once again, with the scheduled concert a complete sell-out, we did a second concert finishing around midnight to accommodate all those who had travelled hundreds of miles to hear us, including some from Lapland.

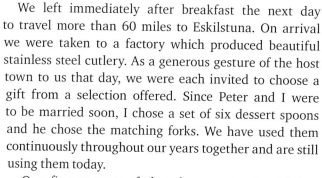

Above and left:
Photo shoot for the
Scandinavian Tour
Below: Sightseeing in
Oslo

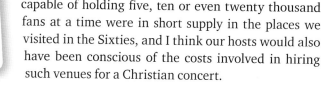

We left immediately after breakfast the next day to travel more than 60 miles to Eskilstuna. On arrival we were taken to a factory which produced beautiful stainless steel cutlery. As a generous gesture of the host town to us that day, we were each invited to choose a gift from a selection offered. Since Peter and I were to be married soon, I chose a set of six dessert spoons and he chose the matching forks. We have used them continuously throughout our years together and are still using them today.

Our first concert of that day was in the Stålfors school auditorium to a very welcoming group of students, before leaving for Örebro, a further 45 miles drive where we were presenting our music in the evening in the Concert Hall, the usual venue for the Swedish Chamber Orchestra. The hall certainly reverberated to a very different kind of music that evening!

The following day saw us facing another very early start and a long drive of almost 200 miles to Gothenburg. After lunch there we played once again to the pupils of a girls' school before giving two concerts in the city's Concert Hall, the first at 7pm and the second beginning at 10pm. It was becoming something of a pattern for our Swedish hosts to schedule two concerts each evening! Built in 1935, Gothenburg Concert Hall is still known as one of the finest concert venues in the world, with the great hall seating 1,247 people. To have sold out two concerts in one night with that many people for a Joystrings presentation tells you something of the way we were received in Sweden. No wonder we went into overdrive for that second late-night concert – our final night in that country.

With the exception of a place like the Royal Albert Hall in London, vast auditoriums or outdoor venues capable of holding five, ten or even twenty thousand fans at a time were in short supply in the places we visited in the Sixties, and I think our hosts would also have been conscious of the costs involved in hiring such venues for a Christian concert.

NORWAY

LEAVING early next morning, we arrived in Sarpsborg five hours later where we were briefed regarding our six-day visit to Norway. After that we were free to relax, enjoy dinner and explore our new surroundings for the rest of the day. Next day we drove a few more miles to Frederikstad and set up our equipment in the Library Hall where, that evening, we gave two concerts. The first was at 7pm and the second started at 9.30pm, meaning that once again we left the concert venue around midnight to return to our hotel.

Thankfully, we did not have to leave for Oslo, a distance of 38 miles northwards, until 10 the next morning. After lunch at the Salvation Army hotel in that city, we drove again a further three hours to Hamar and at 8pm gave a concert in the Hamar Hall. It was on this journey north that we encountered the snow, and none of us could resist stopping the van to enjoy throwing a few snowballs! In Hamar we found that folk from as far away as Bergen and Trondheim had travelled up to 400 miles to be present at our concert that night.

Sunday 7 May was spent at Njard on the outskirts of Oslo, where all of the Salvation Army churches in the city united to share in worship and enjoy music festivals all day and all evening.

On Monday 8 May we presented a concert at 8pm in Drammen Theatre, a little way south-west of Oslo. It was a setting which looked more like an old-time music hall. The stage was set in the centre of a circular block of seats with the boxes rising vertically from the same circumference. In fact we found it quite difficult to speak or sing directly to those in the top tier who only had a bird's-eye view of the stage from a height of 40 feet! The visit of the Joystrings had created such interest that the local daily newspaper ran a three-day series of articles about our work and mission.

The EP *The Song Break* made for our Scandinavian tour had already sold out by now and organisers of the tour were desperately waiting for new orders to arrive.

Tuesday 9 May saw us at Skien, a further 100 miles drive south-east, for a 7.30pm concert in Messehallen, after which we returned to our hotel in Oslo some time after midnight. Our final day was

'The next morning we left for Copenhagen en route for home. During those two weeks on tour in Sweden and Norway we travelled over 3,000 miles, gave 24 concerts, took part in two television performances and reached live audiences of more than 20,000 people'

in Oslo, recording for TV in the morning with two concerts in the evening, one starting at 7pm the other at 9.30pm in the concert hall on Olaf Bulls Plass. The first concert will certainly stand out in our memories for three of us – Peter and Bill and me. Following the introductions to the first concert we were given our promotions from the rank of lieutenant to captain by the Chief Secretary of Norway, Colonel Olav Jakobsen. We were each presented with a full set of extra 'pips' for our shoulder epaulettes, there on the stage.

The next morning we left for Copenhagen en route for home. During those two weeks on tour in Sweden and Norway we travelled over 3,000 miles, gave 24 concerts, took part in two television performances and reached live audiences of more than 20,000 people, our largest single crowd being around 3,000. On the whole, the acceptance of the Joystrings by the Scandinavian people came as a surprise to all those involved. If our group was deemed controversial in terms of outreach ministry by the churches in England, it was even more so in Scandinavian eyes. And yet, in the words of Colonel Jakobsen, 'The Joystrings came, saw and won the hearts of the Scandinavians'.

the Joystrings

TOMORROW ● EWERYTHING

THIS IS LIVING ● IT WON'T ALWAYS BE LIKE THIS

Festival EP 47

Above: Scandinavian EP cover **Above right:** With stand-in drummer, Roger **Right:** Bound for Copenhagen **Left:** Together in Norway

63

Right: Peter and Sylvia's wedding

8

A RIGHT
ROYAL
OCCASION

THE JOYSTRINGS

RETURNING TO LONDON FOLLOWING this exhausting tour, Peter and I had final preparations to make for our wedding. The *London Evening Standard*, the *Daily Mail*, *The Guardian*, *The Daily Record*, the *Surrey Advertiser*, the *Church Times* and other papers all carried as a news item the announcement that we were to be married on 8 July at New Addington Parish Church, Surrey, along with photographs. We had chosen the venue because this was the last district where I had worked for a few months before returning to the group. I got to know the Church of England minister there and the Joystrings had given a concert in the church. Besides, the little Salvation Army hall across the way was not registered for weddings, and in any case would have been far too small for invited guests and members of the press we knew would turn up on the day. However, one of my dear folk in The Salvation Army there provided the buffet reception as a wedding gift, another provided the wedding cake – and yet another provided the photography! What did we have to worry about?

Naturally, there had been much discussion about what would happen to the group after we were married. Invitations were still pouring in, and Peter and I decided it was right for us to carry on with the group. Unlike Ruth and Pauline, who had married before us, Peter and I were together in the Joystrings, so it wasn't the case that one of us was heading off and leaving the other behind! We were to live in fashionable Kennington Road, a row of Georgian terraced houses where, just a few doors away from where we were to live, the great Charlie Chaplin spent his childhood. It was an interesting place and we took great delight in getting the house ready for when we would move in together. I moved in a few weeks before the wedding to finish off the furnishings and I quickly learned where our nearest shops were – up Lambeth Walk.

Our wedding was truly a Joystrings affair. Bill was our best man, Wycliffe gave me away at the altar, and Joy, Wycliffe, and Bill were present at the signing of the register. My bridesmaid was my friend Gillian – we had been students together and have remained firm friends throughout the years.

As expected, on the day the press with their cameras turned up in their droves and had to be marshalled by Bill who did a great job in trying to keep the whole thing dignified. After a wonderful reception we drove off to the beautiful village of Alfriston in Sussex. However, it was only to be a short honeymoon as the Joystrings had been invited to meet Her Majesty the Queen at a Buckingham Palace garden party in mid-July. Briefed as always regarding those guests to be presented, Her Majesty seemed genuinely interested in what the group was trying to do when she spoke with us. She was especially impressed to know that we had been invited to present our music in so many prisons all over the country. She managed to speak with every member of the group, which also included Wycliffe's wife, Liz, and Bill's fiancée, Jean, in conversation. She asked about our music, the lyrics and our busy programme. All in all, I guess Her Majesty spent about eight minutes with us before continuing to speak with others who were being presented.

I should just mention here that an interim engagement between the return from Scandinavia and our marriage was for the Joystrings to visit Queenswood School, Hatfield. It was described as the 'Eton of girls' schools' by the then headmistress, Miss Enid Essame. This was the first time a Salvation Army representation had been to this particular public school, which is built on the site of an estate which once belonged to Sir Thomas More. The girls gathered in the school hall for our concert on that horrendously rainy day and gave us a wonderful welcome.

> 'It was only to be a short honeymoon as the Joystrings had been invited to meet Her Majesty the Queen at Buckingham Palace'

Left: Presented to HM the Queen Elizabeth II **Top right:** Pauline and Joy at the wedding reception **Above:** The wedding party

67

During our time with the girls we were able to speak about our work as a group and our faith as individuals.

Having shared a meal afterwards, we were surprised to hear from staff that by 8.30pm the boarders would have to be in their rooms, and so they wouldn't be able to wave us off. Little did they know…! As we drove around the school buildings on our way out, at every dormitory window of the houses were the girls, waving and shouting their thanks. We did a farewell drive – twice round the circular flower beds – gave two hoots of the horn and then we were off.

Having visited Queenswood we now felt a sense of fulfilment, as we had previously played at the renowned boys' and girls' public schools of Sherborne, Dorset, when on two successive days we gave concerts to 1,200 pupils and staff. Following this, on the Monday morning we attended the famous Sherborne Abbey for school assembly at the headmaster's invitation.

Straight after the garden party at Buckingham Palace we all took a vacation and benefited from a much needed rest. This also gave Peter and me a chance to settle into our new home and get to know the area we were going to be living in. We can hardly

believe now that we were able to walk easily across Lambeth Bridge and on to Victoria, where we could watch a movie or go to the theatre. How we loved living in central London in those days, and somehow the noise of traffic on that busy road didn't bother us at all.

During our first weeks of marriage we bought a pedigree Irish red setter puppy called Captain Barnabas Wendover. We took great delight in walking him to Kennington Park and up Lambeth Walk to our favourite butcher's shop, where he quickly became a favourite customer of the manager. 'Barney', as we nicknamed him, often came with us on some of our more informal Joystrings events, especially when it was to a primary school. The kids loved him as much as we all did.

'During our first weeks of marriage we bought a pedigree Irish red setter puppy called Captain Barnabas Wendover'

Above right: Outside Buckingham Palace, together with Wycliffe's wife, Liz, and Bill's fiancée, Jean **Right:** Sylvia with Captain Barnabas Wendover **Opposite page:** Barney goes to school

Left:
Back in the
spotlight on
tour

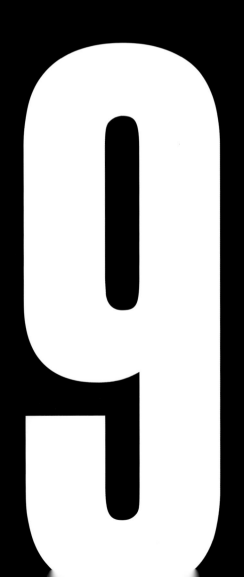

9

ON
THE
ROAD
AGAIN

THE JOYSTRINGS

IT WAS SOON BACK TO WORK AGAIN, and in particular we needed to start rehearsing for a new Christmas LP *Carols Around the World – with the Joystrings*. This took traditional carols from countries like Spain, the Czech Republic, Germany and Australia, and gave them our own arrangements and style.

Our first autumn concert took us to the Bicester Ministry of Defence establishment in Oxfordshire. At first sight we wondered if we had indeed come to the right place. But there, in the middle of what seemed to us disused Nissan huts, was the Garrison Theatre, where we would be presenting our music and our message that evening. Despite our misgivings about the venue we had a great night.

From there we travelled down to Crawley, Sussex, which in the Sixties was indeed a new town. We were a little apprehensive at first, because even when we were setting up to play in the bandstand of the town square there was hardly a person in sight. But our fears about an audience were totally unfounded, for by the time we were ready a crowd of close to 2,000 people were there to listen. We had been well warned by the organisers to make sure that at each hour, on the hour, we should stop playing for four minutes or we would be competing with the magnificent town clock. Naturally we forgot – much to the amusement of the crowd. They must have appreciated our presentation, since there were cries of 'More, more!' and 'Come again!' One person in the crowd wanted us all to go to her place for afternoon tea!

After this engagement we were able to return to our London homes and get a few hours' rest before starting off in the morning for Luton. We were making a return visit to the Vauxhall Motor Works to give two lunch-hour concerts to 6,000 workers. However, to our dismay the van which had been garaged overnight at our London headquarters in Queen Victoria Street simply wouldn't start. A mechanic was called out, but even to his trained mind the van was a non-starter and would have to go for immediate repairs to a nearby garage. By this time we were already behind schedule. Even if we could have found a replacement vehicle it was obvious that we were not going to make it to Luton in time to set up and perform for the workers' lunch break. So, sadly, for the first time in our history, we were unable to make it to a venue.

We were a very apprehensive group that finally left London that afternoon, hoping that the repaired van was really all right for all the travelling we had ahead of us. We were scheduled to present a concert at the College Theatre in Luton that evening, where a very large crowd had gathered. For that concert Wycliffe was allocated a gantry of tubular steel, usually used for changing spotlights, as his drumming stage. He admitted after the concert that being suspended ten feet above the stage, he hadn't really been able to hear the singing too well, but relied on watching Bill's foot tapping throughout to keep him on rhythm!

Unfortunately the rest of the week was a bit of a nightmare with the van which kept breaking down, and at one point we were delayed for three hours at Henley-on-Thames. Thankfully, we still made our appointment at Cheltenham, and that night we gave a concert in the town hall in aid of the Disabled Drivers Association. For Wycliffe, who has specialised all his life in designing or adapting buildings for the disabled, this appeal was close to his heart and a very worthwhile fundraising event.

A DAY IN SCHOOL

AS you will have gathered, it was not unusual for us to be asked to visit a school, such as the Great Sampford Primary School in Essex. However, it was unusual for us to be asked to spend the *entire* day in school, which is what happened when we were invited to Queen Eleanor's School in Hertfordshire. We had a very early start from our London homes because we began by leading the school assembly at 9am. This was followed immediately by joining with the fifth-formers for an hour-long debate in their religious studies class. They certainly knew a lot more about Salvation Army history by the time the class was over.

At 11am we gave a one-hour concert for the junior school, which proved to be such fun and probably the youngest audience we have ever had. Wycliffe managed to augment the percussion

Above: Sylvia shows the pupils of Great Sampford Primary School Bill's Vox guitar

Left: Bill in Bob Dylan mode

side of the group to about 12 in number. Delving into his drum kit he produced castanets, maracas, bongos, a tambourine, shakers, claves and a cowbell. What a noise!

We shared a quick school lunch with the staff at noon, and then went straight into another hour's performance at 1.30pm, this time with the senior school. Finally, we gave a 3pm concert which incorporated the school's Harvest Festival. Invitations had gone not only to the school governors, all the staff, some of the parents and the pupils of the entire school, but also to some specially invited senior citizens from the community. At the end of the festival we helped to distribute the beautiful baskets of fruit, vegetables and provisions to those elderly folk present who would benefit from the school's spirit of caring.

THE WEEK WE SHOCKED THE WORLD

IN mid-October 1967, The Salvation Army in the UK launched a huge public appeal for funding for its social work. Introduced at a big press conference by Major Ken Nutty, Public Relations Secretary at the time, the appeal generated much publicity and led subsequently to the Joystrings' appearance in the most unlikely of places – the Playboy Club in Park Lane, London. Our involvement with such a notorious club was a step too far for many of 'the saints' and it turned out to be the week we shocked the world.

All the daily papers ran with the story and carried huge photographs of Joy and Peter appearing with the 'Bunny girls' who were suitably attired in polo sweaters, mini skirts and bunny ears. They were ready to go out and sell 'Salvation Bonds' at £1 a time at The Royal Exchange and Trafalgar Square in London. This was to be the peak week of The Salvation Army's campaign to raise £3 million towards building 28 new social centres in the UK. The deal with the Playboy Club was that they would give the support of their Bunny girls to the fundraising appeal in exchange for the Joystrings playing at the club for three nights.

The campaign also included the use of dramatic photographs taken by leading photographers such as Lord Snowden and

Above: Stirring the world's biggest Christmas pudding

Below: With Jack Domanio and David Kosoff;

Bunny girl Marta Norgaard with singer Joy Webb, 36, and bass guitarist Peter Dalziel, 25.

THE Salvation Army has infiltrated that temple to the sweet life, the Playboy Club in Park-lane.

Here, to prove it, are two of them getting friendly with a bunny girl.

The Salvationists are singer Joy Webb, 36, and bass guitarist Peter Dalziel, 25, from the Army's pop group, the Joystrings.

Marta the bunny girl, joining in a rather swinging crusade

Below: With Miss World (1966), Reita Faria

Left: Playboy press release in the *Daily Mirror*

75

David Bailey. One of the photographic exhibitions connected with the appeal was opened by the then Miss World, Reita Faria, in Kensington. Those old enough to remember the campaign will also recall that in return for their £1 donors received a big metal badge which bore the inscription 'Be an angel give a £1', and of course the Bunny girls wore these too. The full account of the Joystrings' involvement, how it all happened, why it happened and the reaction to it happening, can be read in the next chapter, 'Attacked and Defended'.

Much of September and October was taken up with rehearsals and time in Abbey Road studios for the release of the LP *Carols Around the World – with the Joystrings*. In addition we had engagements in November, including a concert at the Fairfield Halls in Croydon again, this time in aid of Help the Aged. The next day found us in the Lord Mayor of London's annual show and parade, the theme of the show being 'The Arts'. A few weeks earlier Lord Montagu, on hearing of our invitation to take part in the mayoral procession, had invited us down to Beaulieu in the south of England to choose a vintage car to ride in from his historic collection at the National Motor Museum. The Lord Mayor's Show proved to be a great day out, and we were borne by a 1922 Maxwell 25cwt charabanc. We rode ahead of The Salvation Army's International Staff Band, and though it was a glorious sunny day we were very glad we were being chauffeur-driven rather than having to march all the way like the stoic bandsmen!

Just days later we sang at St Giles Centre, Camberwell, London, for the visit of Her Majesty Queen Elizabeth the Queen Mother. But it was almost like going from the sublime to the ridiculous when three of us, Joy, Peter and I, were then asked as part of the Centenary Appeal fundraising campaign to stir the largest Christmas pudding in the world, weighing over a quarter of a ton. The stirring, using a gigantic wooden spoon, was done on the morning of 27 November at Peek Frean's South London factory. The pudding took two weeks to make and was a gift from the biscuit company to The Salvation Army. When cooked it provided over 2,000 portions – enough to feed every man living in a Salvation Army hostel in London at the time. It was eventually distributed to the recipients by Peek Frean's own staff and members of The Salvation Army.

The giant pudding went on display at Selfridges store in Oxford Street from 7-16 December, was on the *Blue Peter* TV programme on 7 December and finally made it to St Paul's Cathedral steps on 18 December, where at 1pm that day the Joystrings again gave a concert as the climax of the Centenary Appeal. This had to be the most travelled and photographed Christmas pudding ever!

Another Christmas spectacular followed in December when we presented a concert entitled The Joystrings Christmas Package at Clapton Congress Hall along with guest stars Jack de Manio, David Kossoff and Polly Elwes and our friends the children of Great Sampford Primary School. The proceeds of the Christmas concert were going to The Salvation Army's goodwill services – a section of the Army which provided for the needs of people in local communities. We gave another concert at the Queen Elizabeth Hall on 23 December when we were joined by the Wimbledon Girl Singers, the Cantate Domino Boys' Choir from Aalst (a town 30 kilometres from Brussels) and the Kindersingers to present A Festival of Carols and Christmas Music. Present on that occasion was His Excellency the Belgian Ambassador – no doubt there especially to hear the Belgian boys' choir.

A whirlwind of Christmas activities and concerts enabled our new Christmas LP to make good sales everywhere. Somehow in December we even managed to fit in a short visit to South Wales where we played to crowds of people in the Brangwyn Hall, Swansea, which seated over 1,000 people, and the drill hall in Llanelli – an odd choice of venue perhaps, but chosen possibly because it could seat 500 and must have been one of the biggest halls in the town at that time.

On New Year's Eve, when General Frederick Coutts broadcast the *People's Service* on BBC Radio 2 from the Salvation Army hall at Wood Green, London, he used the Joystrings' recording of 'It Won't Always Be like This' – perhaps one of the group's most direct and ever relevant evangelistic songs – to emphasise his New Year message.

Above: On parade at the Lord Mayor's Show.

10

THE JOYSTRINGS

ANY NEW PHENOMENON ALWAYS attracts its critics and its supporters, and the Joystrings had their fair share of both! From the very early days of the group's existence people from both inside and outside the Church wanted to voice their opinions. The attackers wrote about the Joystrings' music, their presentation, the content of 'performances', their image and so on, while the supporters commented on their talent, their professionalism, their dedication to ministering the gospel in new and innovative ways and their ability to communicate to young people in areas where the Church was failing.

Over the five years of the existence of the group, the Joystrings phenomenon always caused debate. What most people don't realise is that the emergence of the Joystrings was not planned or even foreseen. It's worth reiterating that it simply happened as a result of General Frederick Coutts's inaugural press conference in November 1963.

Nor did any of the group members volunteer or apply to be a part of the Joystrings. We were simply selected from the student body of which we were a part while we were at The Salvation Army's International Training College in South London. A chance sighting of guitars in the rooms of two of the male cadets by their house officer, Captain John Larsson, meant that they were possible candidates for an impromptu performance in front of TV cameras. The question of whether or not they could actually play their guitars didn't even arise! In fact, the way this group of young people were launched into a media frenzy is nothing short of a miracle. After initial press photographs, there came the invitation to appear on BBC's *Tonight* programme. This was quickly followed by calls to the BBC switchboard asking to see more of this new group, and there was plenty of response from viewers on the opinion programme *Points of View*. Already, within days of the initial public appearance, there were those attacking and those defending this new approach to musical ministry!

Then came the invitation from the Canadian Broadcasting Company for the group to perform, followed immediately by a phone call from the famous EMI Abbey Road studios in London. The Salvation Army already had a contract with EMI under the Regal Zonophone label and the company wanted to do a test recording with this new group.

'New group'? What was happening? Invitations to hold more press conferences, to appear in clubs, to make recordings – none of this was envisaged or planned. Here was a group of young students and two staff members with a vocational calling, quite literally for Heaven's sake! No one was prepared for this rollercoaster of unprecedented events – not even the Training Principal or the General! But once The Salvation Army had shown that it was happy to try its hand at communicating the gospel in the modern idiom, following the close harmony sound of the Beatles, and having seen the response it stirred among people, who was to say it couldn't continue or that it was not inspired by God's Holy Spirit?

'Playboy Club joins The Salvation Army' – so ran the headlines across British national newspapers in October 1967. It was all part of a fund-raising campaign under the title of 'For God's Sake Care' devised by The Salvation Army's publicity chief of the day, Major Will Pratt, and the Head of International Public Relations, Colonel Arnold Brown. The object of the campaign, as previously mentioned, was to raise £3 million in order to build 28 new social centres in the UK. These were to meet the needs of 400,000 deprived children, 675,000 elderly people and 400,000 socially-challenged people.

The launch reception of the campaign in the VIP suite of the Playboy Club in Park Lane, Mayfair, London, with the reigning Miss World, Reita Faria, and the Joystrings in attendance, was of course designed to attract as much attention as possible to The Salvation Army's appeal. 'We could have held the launch in a cathedral,' said Major Pratt, 'but the impact would not have been the same. What's the point of Christianity which stays behind its comfortable church walls?' The following day ten of the Playboy girls – 'Bunnies' – were selling and autographing £1 Salvation Army bonds outside The Royal Exchange, which had been the centre of commerce for the City of London for many centuries; and these bonds were also sold in Playboy gift shops.

Most unlikely dateline for Salvation Army Press conference:
Playboy Club, London, Monday

AS General Booth might h a v e said : "Why should the Devil have all the best birds ? "

And for the next week the bunny girls of London's Playboy Club will help to raise money for the Salvation Army.

In return, the Army's pop g r o u p, the Joy Strings, will play three nights at the club's discotheque in Park Lane.

From tomorrow until Saturday the bunnies will be at the Royal Exchange, in the City, selling Salvation Army Bonds at £1 a time.

Then they move to Trafalgar Square for four days. At both places

there will be an exhibition of pictures. The theme : "For God's Sake Care."

Above: Playboy press release in the *Daily Mail*
Above right: Salvation bonds for sale

Right: Communicating the message on the cabaret floor
Far right: In the disco with dancing 'bunnies'

The role of the Joystrings in all of this, sanctioned by General Coutts, was to 'perform' in the Playboy Club for three consecutive nights during this fund-raising campaign. The hope was that we would not only entertain but also reach the diners and dancers with our distinctive gospel message. But what a challenge we had been set – to reach one of the most sophisticated and international audiences in London! There was real prayer – God help us!

The Reverend John Lambert of BBC's *Town and Around* radio programme came along on each of the three nights, without his clerical collar, actually to see how badly (he admits) the whole exercise failed. To be honest, we felt our first night was a disaster. We had been asked to play on the discotheque level, where we soon realised we would never make any kind of impact – folks were there to dance, not listen to our songs! After talking with the management it was agreed we should move up to the cabaret level where people sat and actually listened to music. There we could sing songs with more appropriate lyrics suited to our audience, songs like 'It Won't Always Be like This':

Emma, sitting in her rocking chair,
Feeling secure in her Victorian lair,
Lacework lying finished on the dusty shelf,
Poor Emma seventy years herself.

Edward, sitting in director's chair,
Feeling secure with his stocks and shares,
House and home and the best of health,
Here's to Edward and his so-called wealth.

Stocks can fall and chairs can splinter,
Like fading lace, summer turns to winter.
House and home, which once seemed secure,
Are just a memory and exist no more.

Man clinging to the things that fail
Woman depending on a man so frail,
When will they learn that only God is sure?
In him they can find a life secure.

(Words by Peter Dalziel, music by Nigel Robson)

The whole set-up of the Joystrings playing in the Playboy Club was extraordinary. How bizarre it was to see people walking away from the gaming tables in the club, having lost several hundred pounds, only to be faced with a huge display of posters set up by The Salvation Army showing a starving child, a pregnant schoolgirl or the faces of homelessness on our streets. This was a publicity campaign which spoke volumes in no uncertain terms to the ordinary man about town. If the power of the gospel couldn't work here, then it wasn't worth preaching.

One director of a company, in the club for a night out, said that this was certainly the way for the Church to evangelise, and if it continued to do so he would have to become a Christian. I think the Playboy staff and personnel certainly discovered during the week that being a Christian is joyful, meaningful and life-changing. Victor Lownes, the flamboyant founder and manager of the London Playboy Club, said, 'We have moved from the play business into the *pray* business.'

But our appearance at the Playboy Club caused widespread controversy, especially among the saints. The Joystrings were on the brink of an American tour, sponsored by The Salvation Army in the USA. However, when news of the group's appearance at the Playboy Club hit the headlines in the USA, the Salvation Army Headquarters in London was besieged by requests and letters from American Salvation Army officers to 'get them out of that place' saying, 'If you don't get them out of there, their visit to the USA will be in jeopardy' and 'What is a group of young Salvationist musicians doing in such a club?'

It was our wise General Coutts who responded himself to the attacks made upon the Joystrings. He simply said, 'Cancel the tour! The Joystrings are here for the sinners, not the saints!'

Now two years into his term of office, General Coutts felt strongly that he must defend the Joystrings' efforts against such criticisms. Early in our ministry he had written in the Christmas 1965 edition of *The War Cry*:

The mission of The Salvation Army is simple and must be simply stated. It is to take the Christian gospel to the people wherever they are. This can be understood quite

Above: General Coutts defends the Joystrings

literally, for we ourselves act upon it literally. Wherever people are to be found, there we go with the only message that can change character, transform home, redeem society and save the world.

Consequently, those who raise their eyebrows ever so slightly when a group of young Salvationists make an appearance at 'The Blue Angel nightclub' in the heart of London or hold street meetings in Soho on Saturday evenings, cannot have understood the unqualified acceptance of our Saviour's command to preach the gospel to every creature... It follows that we deem it not only allowable, but essential, to use every method congruous with the spirit of the gospel to make it known. 'With the spirit of the gospel' be it noted – for this can be somewhat at variance with the current conventional practice of the gospel.

The Reverend John Lambert, who had come to witness failure, certainly felt that God was present in the midst of those clients of the Playboy Club who sipped their champagne and ate their caviar. He remarked at the time, 'It feels suspiciously like the New Testament approach to me, and just like the central figure of the New Testament, the folks who are brave enough to share the gospel in this way will always be criticised by so called "religious" folks!'

Lambert also went on to say that when the Lord Mayor of London proclaimed the opening of The Salvation Army's fund-raising campaign with the help of the Playboy Bunny girls on the steps of The Royal Exchange on 18 October 1967, a lot of people cheered and a lot of people criticised. He reminded people to remember that the Army has always pioneered in evangelism in places which other Christians might consider shocking or radical – but at least 'they are where the people are'.

The Joystrings never did go to the USA as a group, and sadly we couldn't fulfil our invitation to appear on the famous Ed Sullivan variety TV show to follow in the footsteps of Elvis Presley, the Beatles, the Rolling Stones, the Jackson Five, Bob Dylan and many others. On reflection, perhaps our music and our outreach ministry was too revolutionary for our American friends at the time. But who knows what *could* have happened in our ministry if we had made that tour?

The Sixties were an 'awakening' time in the world. They were exciting, turbulent and revolutionary years which embraced great social and technological changes. There were peace marches and civil rights demonstrations, the space race was on – and who could forget the men who walked on the moon? All kinds of social taboos were being broken, and in the world of television, theatre and film a new freedom in art forms was being established. In addition, young people were finding many new platforms on which to express their own points of view especially through music and fashion. The United Kingdom was exploding with various kinds of creative expression, one of which was the Joystrings!

THOSE FOR AND THOSE AGAINST

COUNTLESS columns in Salvation Army papers and church magazines debated the validity and effectiveness of the Joystrings' ministry over the five years of their existence. Even some of the national newspapers wondered what the Church had got itself into by entering the world of pop music.

We have to admit we didn't always get it right. We were just young, raw recruits in the music business. We had no performance training or experience and, quite frankly, little experience of the world. We learned along the way. Although we prepared our hearts and minds before each event, we knew there were those around the world who were also praying on our behalf.

One critic wrote that he didn't believe we should *entertain* in our presentations: 'Entertaining is for the secular world, not the religious.' Another righteous critic wrote: 'The Joystrings are just entertainers, and anyone who says they have been introduced to Christ by their music is talking nonsense. People who support

this kind of music are not Christians. The Joystrings have been to my church twice but I kept well away on both occasions! What we need in church today is more prayer and Bible study, not worldly entertainment.'

However, another Salvationist wrote: 'I need to apologise to Captain Joy Webb and the Joystrings for my repeated outbursts concerning their music-making. I feared that an extreme "pop" rhythm would infiltrate our Movement and mar the work of our brass band arrangers and composers... now I recognise that my fears were unfounded. The group's arrangements are most pleasant and importantly a great help in introducing younger people to the gospel message.'

Also on the plus side a notable Salvation Army officer wrote: 'It is good to read of the Joystrings' activities. In Britain this group has made a considerable breakthrough in communicating with un-churched people. In places "high" and "low" the subject of the Joystrings is a sure-fire talking point. They present a joyous expression of the faith they hold. After years of trying to persuade folks to attend musical events, it was recently my pleasure to organise a Joystrings concert and have three customers for every ticket available!'

From their workplace someone else wrote: 'One of the girls in my office is a non-believer in the Christian faith. However, last night she heard and saw the Joystrings on television, presenting *Song Break*. She arrived this morning full of praise for their ministry. "Normally," she said, "I would switch off any religious programme, but not this time – they captured my attention for spiritual things for the first time".'

And yet another wrote confessing: 'I am a prodigal. I have been troubled for years about faith, and became an atheist. My journey back to faith has been agonizingly slow. However, lately, when I have been really depressed, it is the music of the Joystrings which has lifted my spirits and brought words of encouragement to me. Their recent visit to my city was a high

'The United Kingdom was exploding with various kinds of creative expression, one of which was the Joystrings!'

point in my life. Believe me when I say that although you may not care for their music or their presentation, they are helping many people in their spiritual journey. Incidentally I am a music teacher and can vouch for their high standard of musicianship.'

One editor, in response to his postbag of mail regarding the ongoing Joystrings debate, wrote: 'The Joystrings are specialists, earnest missionaries, reaching out especially to young folks and using the historic Salvation Army technique of speaking and singing in terms which will be understood by those they are seeking to reach with their message. They are not here to primarily bless the saints!'

LETTERS FROM PRISON

FOLLOWING a concert given by the Joystrings at Shepton Mallet Prison in March 1967, a letter arrived on Joy's desk with the signatures of many of the prisoners who were present on that occasion. It read:

> *Will you please accept this letter as an expression of our appreciation for your visit here on Sunday? Your music and singing made a great impression on all of us, but an even greater impression was made by your faith and sincerity, both of which were radiantly obvious.*
>
> *We extend to you our sincerest thanks and hope you will visit again in the near future.*

There also appeared in a local church newspaper the personal testimony of a young man. Describing his involvement with soft drugs and his experiences in a mental institution, he told how his life changed after watching and listening to the Joystrings present their faith and message through their music on television. He destroyed his heroin and had not used drugs since.

In April 1967 some prisoners in France wrote to The Salvation Army in Britain asking if anyone could supply them with the words and music of the Joystrings' songs. Apparently they had seen us perform on French TV and those who were interested in pop music wanted to get hold of our material.

Wycliffe was very grateful for the mechanical training given to young offenders at Guys Marsh Prison in Dorset when, within a space of 20 minutes, the car mechanic squad had fixed a puncture on his MG which he had parked just outside the gates! It was here that 600 young men packed into their little theatre listened so intently to everything we sang and said. Who can judge just how far-reaching our ministry was to anyone of those young men gathered there?

A TIME FOR REJOICING

SOMEONE else wrote: 'I've had reservations about the Joystrings and I have heard and read many more, but after their recent visit to my city I am only sorry they cannot manage more engagements. Their presentation of the gospel was crystal clear – attractive, unemotional and it appealed to all ages, judging by the response they received. Almost 1,000 people were present at the City Hall to hear them. And if we were to count the number of new Christians or revived Christians as a result of their ministry I am certain our Lord is rejoicing!'

In January 1967, The Salvation Army's youth magazine, *Vanguard*, carried a debate between young people on the validity of allowing such a group to operate within the Church. Much of the debate followed arguments of those for and those against, with their various reasons. Finally the chairman offered some pertinent facts:

> *No group so small has ever made such a spiritual impact around the world, in the history of The Salvation Army.*
>
> *Seven cadets were currently training to become full-time Salvation Army officers that year as a direct result of the Joystrings' ministry.*
>
> *Thousands of people are recorded as seeking spiritual direction for their lives in every year of the Joystrings' musical evangelism.*
>
> *Through the group, The Salvation Army is able to reach into areas and arenas of people usually forbidden*

to the Church.

A massive breakthrough in the world of television, recording and theatre presentation, all in the name of spiritual ministry, has been made in a very short time.

This calls for rejoicing!

DEFENDED BY HISTORY

IN April 1964, when the newly formed Joystrings had just played in the Blue Angel nightclub in Soho, London, Major Brindley Boon, then Head of the Music Department for The Salvation Army in the UK and under whose jurisdiction the Joystrings came in May 1965, wrote about creative evangelism in the early days of The Salvation Army:

There have been other 'Joy Strings' [sic], who have sought to be 'with it' in their day and commended themselves to the heart of [our Founder] William Booth, who was always conscious of the need for new methods to meet the demands of new problems.

In April 1878, before The Christian Mission became The Salvation Army, a letter in the Salisbury and Winchester Journal signed 'Disgusted', called the attention of the readers to the disgraceful scene which took place in the city every Sunday when 'disorderly characters paraded the streets singing revivalist hymns, which were freely interspersed with yells, whistling and comic songs'. Later that year the appearance of four brass instrumentalists in the market-place of that same city brought further annoyance to the respectable inhabitants, but did not prevent Charles Fry and his three sons from pioneering a work which expanded into the largest amateur music-making organisation in the world.

Unusual methods and the widespread use of unusual musical instruments reaped a rich harvest as the 'godless masses' became arrested by this different approach to the gospel message. [...]

Army leaders were quick to utilise this means of effective pioneering. When it was decided to launch the work of

the Army in Marylebone [...] Captain Eliza Haynes was appointed to lead the salvation onslaught.

Captain Haynes was known far and wide as 'Happy Eliza'. In Nottingham her unusual methods of attracting the attention of citizens were successful. When attempts to begin operations had left the people unmoved, she decided to create interest by dashing through the streets with a banner, 'Happy Eliza', streaming from her hair. Later she was marching along the same streets beating time [to the music] with her 'fiddle stick' [violin bow ...], while a procession [...] sang the songs of salvation.

It was no surprise when, to draw a crowd at Marylebone, 'Happy Eliza' appeared in the Edgware Road neighbourhood sitting on the box seat of a four-wheeler cab attracting attention by playing her fiddle.

The fame of 'Happy Eliza' quickly spread. She became the subject of music-hall songs; comedians in Christmas pantomimes, dressed for the part, mimicked her, and dolls, toys and sweets were named after her.

The War Cry, 4 April 1964, p.5.

In March 1880 an order was issued by the leaders of The Salvation Army for as many officers and soldiers as possible to obtain and learn to play all manner of musical instruments in order to aid the salvation war. Any friends of the Army who had instruments not being used could send them to the Army's headquarters for distribution. Violins, bass viols, concertinas, drums, brass instruments or anything else which could make a joyful noise unto the Lord would be welcomed!

So it was that all kinds of novel variations of musical groups came into being in the early days of the Army. As Boon continued in his article:

Writing in an American musical journal in 1930, John Philip Sousa said: 'Music, even in its most primitive forms, seems to have an influence upon some portion of mankind. The Salvation Army, for instance, has depended upon banjos, accordions, guitars,

Above: Original Joystrings! **Right:** First line-up at the Blue Angel Nightclub

tambourines – anything that was musical – to spread the gospel.' This was an acknowledgement, from a qualified source, that the brass band was not the Army's only effective medium.

In some countries where stringed instruments have always held prior place the present British 'craze' is hard to understand. When Army activity began in France no open-air meetings were permitted. Some other method of reaching the people had to be found. One point of contact was established when a band of five women cadets began visiting cabarets, distributing papers, singing salvation songs and inviting the patrons to Army meetings.

The Joy Strings, in taking the gospel message in modern music to The Blue Angel Club [...] are merely following a time-honoured practice that has never really died out in some theatres of salvation war.

The early days of the Army encouraged the 'lone-star'

to apply his talent to the idiom of the day. [...]

Times have changed and a public conditioned to regular TV and radio 'pop' shows, hit parades and beat rhythms is bound to be 'choosy' in its tastes. This makes the unqualified success of 'It's an Open Secret' all the more commendable. A record cannot reach the charts merely by wishful thinking.

We must congratulate these competent young Salvationists [the Joystrings] and their promoters. We must also pray that their spiritual impact will be even more pronounced as they play on the steps of St Paul's Cathedral next month and later take their scintillating beat music and captivating personal testimony into the factory canteens, theatres, dance halls and holiday camps and on the beaches of England's thickly populated resorts.

The Joy Strings are following in a great tradition!

The War Cry, 4 April 1964, p.5.

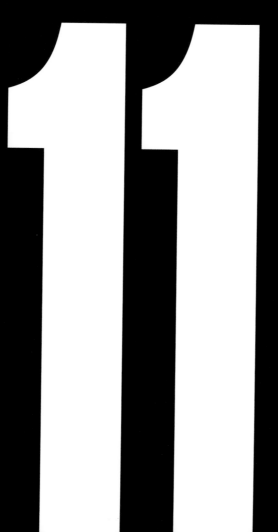

11

BEHIND
THE
SCENES

THE JOYSTRINGS

IN OCTOBER 1965 THE JOYSTRINGS were scheduled to go into Abbey Road studios to record another batch of songs for a new EP to support a forthcoming overseas tour. When we arrived at the studios we were amazed to find Ringo's drums (two sets of them) stacked in a corner. In addition there were several guitars and a sitar – remember that famous Indian instrument used in the Beatles' recording of 'Norwegian Wood'? We were told the Beatles had been in the studios recording until late the night before. This was confirmed by our own producer Walter Ridley who had spent the whole of the previous evening recording with the 'Fab Four'. No wonder he was tired!

Peter and Bill had recorded their own duo composition 'Love That's in My Heart' – a track that sounded very like the Beatles' style. 'Thanks, boys,' said Walter. 'That sounded just like John and Paul. Let's hope it sells as well!'

None of us will forget the time we were in Trafalgar Square for the switching on of the Christmas lights in 1964. The lights were on the traditional Norwegian fir tree donated each year to London. This year the event was being televised, and for us it would be the first public airing of our new single 'A Starry Night'. It was a bitterly cold winter's night and we, along with the Hollies, Brian Poole and the Tremeloes and other groups, were performing to a huge crowd who had gathered for the event. We were all chilled to the bone as we waited during seemingly endless hours of rehearsal. With the conditions being so wintry, we girls had brought along flasks of coffee and tea to stave off the chill of the night, and found ourselves happy to share a cup with some of the guys from the other groups.

And what a thrill it was when, sometime mid-1966, again in Abbey Road studios during another recording session, Walter Ridley asked, 'Would you like to hear the playback?' Of course we would. It was a surprise to us when from the speakers came the newly recorded number 'Bus Stop' by the Hollies. Apart from the artistes and the recording engineers, I think we were the first to hear this number, obviously bound for the charts.

At the beginning of 2011 Reg Presley of the Troggs told *The One Show* that his 1967 hit single 'Love is All Around' was inspired by a Salvation Army pop group. In an interview with the BBC One TV magazine programme the singer explained that seeing the Joystrings on television prompted him to write the song, which carried the same title as one of the Joystrings' songs. Reg said: 'The Joystrings were doing their bit with the tambourine about love, love, love. And it left me with this thing: "I feel it in my fingers; I feel it in my toes." I got the bass out and tapped around on it and I thought, "Whoah! It just felt right".' Wet Wet Wet's version of 'Love is All Around' spent 15 weeks at No 1 in the singles chart in 1994 after it was featured in the film *Four Weddings and a Funeral*.

OUR EXECUTIVE OFFICERS

WELL, 'Executive Officer' was their official title, but we often referred to them as our liaison managers! Thank heavens for Captain Sandy Morrice and Major Peter Hawkins. Our travels would not have been the same without these men. They were the fall guys for anything that had to be sorted, arranged, changed or whatever. They were there to check all the schedules, bookings, places to stay and so on. Looking back we recognise they carried tremendous responsibility, and we guess that at the time we never really gave them full credit for all that they did to smooth our journey as a group.

For each of them, this was not a position they volunteered for. They were appointed by the leaders of The Salvation Army to this role. As with us, these guys were suddenly thrust into the limelight of press and media – they introduced us, they covered at the beginnings of concerts if we were not ready (like the time Bill had left his Salvation Army uniform jacket in the van parked at the landward end of a seaside pier, when we were playing in the pier pavilion, discovering his mistake just minutes before the concert was scheduled to open! Captain Sandy Morrice did a brilliant job in covering for about five minutes, by which time Bill arrived back breathlessly to launch into our opening number of the night.)

Our liaison managers were present at every function throughout the day, often fronting for us when our strength was ebbing and putting on a gracious smile even though they were hearing the same musical repertoire over and over again when we were on tour.

EQUIPMENT

IN the very early days of the group, we used a local South London sound company, R.G. Jones, from which to hire the PA equipment we needed. Three acoustic guitars, a string bass and Wycliffe's drum kit formed the basis of instrumentation. That was it!

It was only when it was realised that the group was going to continue that any serious thought was given to providing some good equipment and having our own amplification system. It was then that the Salvation Army International Headquarters Public Relations team came into play. Brilliant at their job, Major Will Pratt and Major Ken Nutty used all their knowledge and connections, together with all the publicity surrounding this new Salvation Army group, to get sponsorship for equipment.

Within no time at all, the Vox company agreed to sponsor the Joystrings. Formerly known as Jennings Musical Instruments (JMI) of 100 Charing Cross Road, London, Vox was by now heavily into making guitar amplifiers used by such groups as the Shadows. In July 1960 the Shadows had reached number one with their first instrumental recording 'Apache', which featured the sound of Vox AC15 amps, later upgraded to AC30s. In September 1962 the Beatles had recorded 'Love Me Do' and 'How Do You Do It?' using Vox amplifiers, and in October 1962 'Telstar' by the Tornadoes went to the top of the UK charts. Its characteristic riff was played on a Univox organ. Also in the charts that week were Bert Weedon, Lonnie Donegan, the Shadows and the Beatles – all Vox users.

By 1964 Vox had become known as the best of British amplifiers. In return for their sponsorship we provided publicity for their equipment at all our concerts and included amps in the photo shoots. It was a great deal, with both the Joystrings and the company name of Vox aiming to get as much mileage out of it as possible!

Vox also made electric guitars. At first their range included budget guitars based on Fender shapes. But by October 1961 company boss Tom Jennings decided that Vox guitars needed their own shape, style and identity, and commissioned something unique and previously unseen. With a radical trapezoid body, it was brought out as the Phantom, and became an icon of '60s guitar design, soon followed by the Teardrop shape as used by Brian Jones of the Rolling Stones. The Vox Continental Organ made its debut in 1962. With its characteristic orange colour and reversed black and white keys it was an instant classic, used by many of the British groups including the Animals and the Beatles – and by the Joystrings. Played by Joy, this important bit of Joystrings equipment can be seen on photographs of the group performing.

We do consider we were extremely fortunate to have been sponsored by Vox – yet another pointer to the fact that the evolution of the Joystrings at the time when pop music was coming into its own belonged to a much higher authority.

Later in the group's existence Bill moved on to a Rickenbacker guitar as used by John Lennon and Nigel played a Gretsch 'Country Gentleman' as used by George Harrison, while Peter played a Hofner 'violin' bass guitar as used by Paul McCartney. Now where did the influence to use those instruments come from, I wonder!

Sadly Tom Jennings lost control of the Vox company and left it in 1967, but continued as Jennings Electronic Industries to supply equipment to The Salvation Army for a few years from his old Dartford factory.

ROYALTIES

MOST Salvationists, and certainly all Salvation Army officers, will know that all performance fees, royalties or any donations made for any presentation by the Joystrings was money which went directly to The Salvation Army to be used for its work. Any continuing royalties from our music also continues to be used in that way. There never was, nor has there ever been, any thought that any of us would personally benefit financially from the time we spent as members of the group. The copyright of all our music has also stayed within The Salvation Army.

Top left: Joy on the VOX Continental organ
Above: Peter's Hofner violin bass
Above left: With the sound guys from
R.G.Jones **Left:** Peter Hawkins
Far left: Sandy Morrice
Right: Bill and the Gretsch

'Reg Presley of the Troggs told The One Show that his 1967 hit single "Love is All Around" was inspired by a Salvation Army pop group'

Right: First recording at Abbey Road studios

JOYSTRINGS
Christmas Collection

JOYSTRIN

Restru

12

—
IN
RECORD
TIME
—

THE JOYSTRINGS

THERE CAN'T BE MANY PEOPLE WHO haven't heard of EMI's famous recording studios at Abbey Road, London. The Beatles made 90 per cent of their recordings in Studio Two there. In April 1969, they came together to record their final album as a group and called it *Abbey Road*. The sleeve featured the now iconic image of the zebra crossing outside the studios on the front cover, putting Abbey Road on the map once and for all and persuading EMI to give the studios that name. In fact, anyone who logs on to Earthcam on the internet today can see that every minute of every day people are willing to risk life and limb in order to be photographed on that famous pedestrian crossing. In seven years the Beatles made records there which established them as the most successful pop group in the history of recording.

The list of other artists who also passed through the doors of the studios in Abbey Road during the 1960s grew almost daily, among them Cliff Richard, the Shadows, Manfred Mann, Gerry and the Pacemakers, the Seekers, the Hollies, Cilla Black, even Morecambe and Wise – and the Joystrings!

The late Walter Ridley was the Joystrings producer at Abbey Road. He wrote in 1973:

My first meeting with the Joystrings took place in Number 3 studio…. For most of my recording career I have been used to listening to songs brought to me by writers or music publishers' representatives and then making an informed decision which recording artist would be best suited to whatever song I felt was worth recording. After matching artiste(s) to song, I would have an arranger come to me to decide on the kind of musical backing required. Following this a date was set for the recording.

None of this procedure applied to the Joystrings, who when they first came to the studios, did not even have a group name. They went by the title of International Training College String Band Rhythm Group! In fact that's how they appeared on Cliff Michelmore's BBC evening news programme, Tonight. After their first appearance…

the great British public clamoured to see more of these guitar-playing Salvationists. It was after their second TV appearance that an EMI executive asked, 'What are we doing about this little lot?'

Abbey Road's repertoire manager at the time, Robert Dockerill, decided to invite this novel group to the studios to do what was supposed to be a 'test' recording. As the producer I had no idea what songs the group were going to sing and only a vague idea what instruments they would be using, so it was with some trepidation that I arrived at the studios…

Thankfully it turned out wonderfully well! Joy Webb had written 'It's an Open Secret' which, although a test recording, we decided to release and it went straight into the charts. On the flip side another foot tapping number 'We're Going to Set the World a-Singing' was recorded.

After that success we went on to repeat the experience on many subsequent occasions.

Walter Ridley went on to say, years later, that when the Joystrings walked through the doors of Abbey Road recording studios that November, the face of religious music changed for ever. We had hit a new level in communicating the gospel!

These are a couple of the press cuttings for the Joystrings recordings at the beginning of 1964:

'There's only one record that's had more publicity than 'It's an Open Secret' and that's 'She Loves You' by the Beatles'

EMI producer

'The biggest revolution in Britain's record business'
News of the World

Above: Early morning film shoot for German TV in Soho

THE RECORDINGS

SINGLE (RZ501) 1964
It's an Open Secret (Joy Webb)
Set the World a-Singing (Joy Webb)

EP (ERZ8255) 1964
The Joystrings
Trumpet of the Lord (arr. Joy Webb)
Walk in the Light (arr. Joy Webb
When Jesus Comes to You (Joy Webb)
Yes Indeed (Handel Everett)

SINGLE (RZ503) 1964
A Million Songs (Joy Webb)
Joshua (Trad)

SINGLE (RZ504) 1964
A Starry Night (Joy Webb)
Now I Know (Dalziel/Davidson)

EP (ERZ8258) 1965
Have Faith in God
Have Faith in God (Joy Webb)
I Want to Sing It (Joy Webb)
There Was a Man (Joy Webb)
Follow (Joy Webb)

SINGLE (RZ505) 1965
All Alone (Dalziel/Davidson)
He Cares (Joy Webb)

SINGLE (RZ506) 1965
The Only One (Peter Dalziel)
You're Welcome (Joy Webb)

EP (ERZ8260) 1965
Christmas with the Joystrings
This Little Boy (Bill Davidson)
What Dreams (Bill Davidson)
Such a Tiny Child (Joy Webb)
Winter's Coming On (Bill Davidson)

EP (ERZ8261) 1966
Joystrings Abroad
Lord on Our Side (Bill Davidson)
Time (Bill Davidson)
Love That's in My Heart (Dalziel/Davidson)
Without Him (Sylvia Gair)

LP (SLRZ4016) 1966
Well Seasoned
Keep Me in Your Love (Dalziel/Davidson)
He is Near (Joy Webb)
No Time to Lose (Nigel Robson)
Where Will it End? (Peter Dalziel)
Long Lost Cause (Bill Davidson)
Friend for You (Peter Dalziel)
There Will Be God (Joy Webb)
Love That's All Around (Bill Davidson)
We Three Kings (Trad.)
Silent Night (Gruber)
The Little King Jesus (Wiggins/Ingles)
O Little Town of Bethlehem (Brooks/Redner)
Away in a Manger (Luther/Kirkpatrick)
Mary's Boy Child (Haireston)
Do You Hear What I Hear? (Regney/Shane)
The Holly and the Ivy (Trad.)

EP (ERZ8264) 1967
The Song Break
Tomorrow (Bill Davidson)
Everything (Bill Davidson)
This is Living (Bill Davidson)
It Won't Always Be like This (Dalziel/Robson)

LP (SLRZ4018) 1967
Carols Around the World
Once in Royal David's City (Gauntlet/Alexander)
I Saw Three Ships (Trad.)
Czech Rocking Carol (Czech Trad.)
Across the Plains (Australian)
Dance of the Shepherds (Ancient Basque)
On a Dark Night (Korean)
God Rest ye Merry, Gentlemen (Trad.)
Hurry Shepherds (Puerto Rican)
Rise Up Shepherds (African-American)
Hush, Hush, Hush (Austrian)
Carol of the Bagpipers (Italian)
Just be Grateful (Bill Davidson)

Above: Full house at *De Doelen*, Rotterdam

13

THE
BEGINNING
OF THE END

THE JOYSTRINGS

THE FIRST WEEKEND OF FEBRUARY 1968 was spent at Kingston upon Thames. It was a special weekend organised by our drummer Wycliffe who, with his wife Liz, were very much a part of the Salvation Army church and community of Kingston. It began on Friday evening with the group playing at the Cellar Youth Club. The next day, having set up our equipment at the Coronation Hall in Kingston, we were received by the mayor and civic dignitaries in a reception at the Guildhall. Later that evening we gave a concert to a packed audience.

Wanting to make the most of our visit to his home town, Wycliffe had arranged for us to lead a service at St Andrew's Church on Ham Common, and then move on to HM Detention Centre, also on the Common, where we gave a concert for the inmates there. After a very quick lunch we moved on to Gypsy Hill Teacher Training College, where Liz had been a student. There, after giving an afternoon concert, we were able to have an impromptu discussion with the students about our work and music and its relevance to the young people of the day.

Later that Sunday evening we gave a presentation of *The Folk Gospel*, written and inspired by Wycliffe and already used to great effect in the TV service broadcast from New Silksworth Church the previous year.

The Joystrings' only visit to Northern Ireland was a weekend spent at Lurgan in April of that year. Following a mayoral reception the group played to a capacity crowd in Lurgan Town Hall. It was a pity there wasn't a bigger venue available for the occasion because not everyone who wanted to be there could get in. Sunday afternoon saw us playing to the inmates of the women's prison and the boys' borstal at Armagh, and then a final gathering in the Salvation Army worship hall. Once again, although extra seating had been brought in, many people had to be turned away because the hall just wasn't big enough! We put on an extra performance for all the young people who stayed behind later on Sunday evening, before leaving to embark on an overnight ferry back to England. This was a short but memorable visit.

FRANCE

EACH of us embarked upon this 1968 springtime tour with strange feelings in our hearts since we knew this was going to be our last tour ever as a group. Discussions had been going on for weeks about our future – after all, we had been 'on the road' for almost five years! Peter and I had been married for nine months and virtually lived out of a suitcase for most of that time. Bill was engaged to Jean, who was shortly to be ordained and commissioned as a Salvation Army officer, and they were getting married in June of this year. Since Jean was not in the Joystrings it would mean that, if we continued as a group, she would be left on her own a great deal when we were travelling. Not a good start to any marriage! Therefore, between ourselves and the Salvation Army leaders it was decided that this would be our last big tour, and those of us who were officers would receive new appointments at the end of May. But we would continue to fulfil Joystrings engagements through to July, when we would take part in a great rally at Crystal Palace and then be disbanded.

On 30 April we were scheduled to give a concert at 8.30pm in a Protestant church in the city of Lille. Having been delayed at

Above: On stage in Lille, France

Left: Playing to the Dutch Air Force *Kadetschool*
Below: Wycliffe and Liz

customs we were an hour late in arriving in Lille, and the people assigned to meet us had given up and gone home! Eventually, having found the dimly lit church ourselves, we set up and presented our music and message to a very warm, enthusiastic crowd of young people. We finished the concert at 10.45pm but no one wanted to leave. Many of the audience remained to watch us pack up our equipment.

Supper was taken at the Salvation Army men's hostel in Lille somewhere between midnight and 1am on May 1 before moving on to our place of rest for the night. Thankfully, we didn't have to be up at the crack of dawn the next day which was a public holiday in France, because we were giving another concert in Lille that evening in *La Salle du Conservatoire*. There extra chairs had to be squeezed in until 600 people were seated, and there were more standing throughout the evening. (Health and safety officials today would have had a nightmare in some of our venues!) It was a marvellous evening, with one of the most responsive and spontaneous audiences we ever encountered during our existence as a group. There seemed to be no language barrier at all and there were encores demanded for the songs we sang in French. Eighteen young people responded during the singing of the Joystrings prayer songs, wanting to find the

Christian faith for themselves.

The next day we drove to Paris where we were staying at the *Palais de la Femme*, The Salvation Army's women's hostel, a place we were very familiar with from our previous visits to France. After a quick lunch we were formally welcomed to France by Her Majesty's British Consul at the British Embassy, and that evening we gave a concert in The Salvation Army's Central Corps hall for the young resident students of the *Palais de la Femme*, those of the young men's hostel and the local Salvation Army teenagers – in total more than 500 young people. The whole of the first half of the concert was televised and broadcast throughout France the next day. Apart from the music, it was obvious that these young folk had really caught the vision of the message, because 33 of them came forward in response to the Christian challenge. Once again it was after midnight before we finally made it to bed, only to have to be up at 6am the next day to drive 500 kilometres to Lyon in southern France.

We had already been forewarned that it was difficult to get much of a crowd in Lyon, even to so-called important events, so we were dismayed to learn that we were to give a concert in the *Palais d'Hiver* (the Winter Palace) which seated over 2,000 people! What were our hosts thinking of, putting us in this huge music hall where many of the world's most famous stars had played, including the Beatles? However, our fears turned out to be unfounded when 2,800 mostly young people crowded into that venue – some of them being the usual clientele who visited the *Palais* for other events. Essentially we think they came just to see what this novel Christian group was all about. But afterwards the manager said he had never known such an appreciative and attentive audience. Sadly the *Palais d'Hiver* was demolished in 1988 so that a new office area could be developed.

Early press reports the following day in *Le Progrès* and the Catholic papers expressed amazing understanding and appreciation of our deeper motives. One report ran: 'The Joystrings, if they had no message as such, would certainly be among the top-rated groups from Britain at this time, but they are already professionals of the Faith'.

On Sunday morning, 5 May, we conducted a service in the

Above: Brussels TV studio

Salvation Army centre at La Villette and in the afternoon at *La Salle Centrale*, while in the evening we gave a full concert in *La Salle Gaveau* in central Paris. This magnificent concert hall, superbly decorated, built in 1907, seats 1,000 people on three levels. The applause for our presentation was incessant on this occasion, even after we had left the stage for the interval. The concert which began at 9pm did not end until 11.45pm and even then no one wanted it to end – nor did we. The atmosphere was electric! Since the hall was on three levels it was difficult to invite people to respond and accept the Christian faith by coming forward, but folk did just stand where they were or in the aisles and wait for a Christian counsellor to reach them. Among those who stood was a young Jesuit priest who simply wanted to identify with others who stood, and in that moment he rededicated his own life for service.

BELGIUM

TUESDAY 7 May was to be the first and only day we were to present our music in the great European city of Brussels. But it had been arranged so that we would contact as many people as possible in the 24 hours we had there. In the morning we recorded a half-hour programme for radio, when we spoke

Above: Charmed by our Dutch hosts

'The Joystrings, if they had no message as such, would certainly be among the top-rated groups from Britain at this time, but they are already professionals of the Faith'

Above: *La Salle Gaveau*, Paris

about our work, motives, vocation and our place in the world of pop music. The programme went on air at 4pm that day on the *World of Pop* when the maximum numbers of young people were tuned in. Lunch was taken at Waterloo, where we had a chance to recap on our British history and marvel at the panoramic oil painting of this historic battleground. In the afternoon we made a television recording, again lasting half an hour, to be screened the following month. This included eleven Belgian children coming into the TV studios to give atmosphere to a couple of our songs.

The evening performance in Brussels, held in the beautiful *Salle de la Madeleine* concert hall, was an absolute sell-out, and the enthusiasm and fervour we felt there certainly matched those of the French audiences. With the hall packed to capacity and people standing, there was no room at the end of the concert for anyone to make any kind of physical response to our message; we could only pray that we had touched many hearts that night. The evening was further complicated by the fact that we had a television crew filming the whole time, with their additional lighting which boosted the temperature to over 80 degrees Fahrenheit on stage.

It was an amazing day, with two TV recordings, a radio recording, and a full concert. In those few hours we reached thousands of people with our music and Christian message.

THE NETHERLANDS

CROSSING the border from Belgium, we were met at Breda by our Dutch translator, Major Jo Heijnsdijk and other Salvation Army representatives and taken to Rotterdam for lunch and a press conference with reporters from the Dutch national newspapers. From there we continued on to Arnhem, where we set up our equipment in the *Musis Sacrum* in the town square. Once again every one of the 1,000 tickets available was sold and the audience were overwhelming in their warm response to our presentation.

Thursday 9 May was to prove an incredibly exciting and enlightening day for the Joystrings. In the morning we went to the *Luchtacht Kadetschool* (officers training school for the Dutch Air Force) where we gave two concerts, each of one hour duration, with 500 young officer cadets in each, together with a Commander-in-Chief and other staff officers present. Among the staff was a colonel who was considered to be one of the most famous air force pilots

Above: An impromptu concert in the Leeuwarden school

in the world at that time, having been awarded the Dutch Flying Cross three times. Speaking to us after the concerts he said he felt it necessary in his position to know what young people enjoyed and that he especially enjoyed pop music!

Never before had we experienced such appreciation for our music and spoken word – it was moving to see these young men rise en masse to give us a standing ovation. We continued playing for as long as time would allow before sharing lunch with the officers in their staffroom.

That evening we gave a concert to 1,000 people, among whom were the Commander-in Chief of the air force officer cadet school,

together with his wife and family. That night 75 people responded to our invitation to accept the Christian faith for themselves.

By now we were feeling very weary, but we moved on to Amsterdam, carried somewhat by the momentum of all that was waiting for us. On Friday morning we were once again in the TV studios where we worked on recordings till well into the afternoon. That evening our concert was held in the Krasnapolsky Theatre Hall, seating over 1,000 people. This audience seemed to us very noisy, but it transpired that lots of people were simultaneously translating for those who could not understand English as we introduced our songs.

After Amsterdam came Rotterdam, and what for us was the greatest auditorium we had played in on the continent – *De Doelen* – with 2,500 tickets sold for that evening. The afternoon of that day was interesting too. It was advertised as a 'Combo Festival' when Salvation Army groups from all over the Netherlands – groups which had begun as a result of the Joystrings – came and performed at *De Doelen* for over two hours. It was the duty of the Joystrings members to act as judge and jury and give helpful advice on their presentation.

The memory of that evening concert will live with each of us for ever. For sure, this was one of the best public audiences to receive us in the Netherlands. But perhaps the most poignant moment came when a woman dressed in a beautiful glittering evening dress, and her husband who was wearing a tuxedo, walked hand in hand down the aisle and responded to our invitation to accept the Christian faith in their life. They told us afterwards that they had been on their way to a theatre when they saw crowds of people going into *De Doelen*. They changed their minds about the theatre and came instead to our concert – their very first Salvation Army gathering and a life-changing experience for them.

Moving on to The Hague the next day, which was a Sunday, we found ourselves in *De Dierentuin* Concert Hall and Theatre. This was in the grounds of the city zoo, where in the afternoon we gave one of the last concerts ever to be given in this fine old building, to 1,300 people. Despite efforts of a citizens' group to save the concert hall and the zoo, it closed on 30 June later that year and was demolished to make way for new government buildings. This happened just six weeks after our performance there.

On Monday evening we played in the Tivoli, Utrecht – a strange old hall, designed like an aircraft hanger, which made sound very difficult. Nevertheless we managed to create a real concert atmosphere and the crowd responded well.

From Utrecht we travelled north to Assen where our first engagement was to play to more than 1,000 soldiers at a military garrison. After that we moved straight on to Groningen to give a concert in Harmonie Hall to another 1,000 people. The hotel assigned to us was in the middle of the town square where a fairground had been set up. We were lulled to sleep sometime after midnight by the sound of music and merrymaking!

Wednesday 15 May, while we were still on tour, was a significant day for Bill, Peter and me. We each received an official piece of paper which told us what our appointments would be after the Joystrings disbanded. When you realise how much we had been travelling, how much energy we needed to sustain the kind of programme we were following, and the responsibility we all carried for this constant high-profile public ministry, you will understand why it was decided by us and by our Salvation Army leaders that to continue at such a pace indefinitely was unsustainable. Realistically, it was also going to be better if we made the decision to disband the group while we at the top of our form, rather than allow the danger of other elements to creep in and sap our energy. It was a very hard decision to come to, especially when this last tour was drawing sell-out crowds and hundreds of people were responding to the music and message we presented.

We were in Leeuwarden that day and the original proposal for us to give a concert in the town square had to be cancelled because of torrential rain. We went instead to a nearby technical school and gave an impromptu concert to the boys, who didn't seem to mind the terrible weather at all! The rain continued unabated through to the evening concert. To make matters worse, the European Cup football match between Manchester United and Real Madrid was televised from 8.30pm to 10.15pm – the exact duration of our concert. Everyone knows the Dutch are mad about football (and there was no possibility of recording TV broadcasts at home in those days). However we still managed a crowd of 600, and I remember Bill updating the audience every now and again with the football score, which somehow was relayed to us, so that the audience present wouldn't miss out.

So concluded the final tour of the Joystrings. It included 23 public performances, five television appearances and several radio broadcasts, as well as travelling almost 2,000 miles in 17 days. More than 200 people we know of responded publicly to the invitations given to accept the Christian faith – and who knows how many more responded in their hearts?

14

FINAL DAYS

THE JOYSTRINGS

WE RETURNED TO LONDON AFTER the Europe tour knowing we were now approaching the final days of the group. Although we still had some engagements to fulfil, three of us had our sights set on other places. Peter and I were going to live and work in Wokingham, Berkshire, at the end of May; and Bill, together with Jean following their marriage on 8 June in Bath, would be going to Streatham Vale in South London.

Joy was going to continue in the Music Department at Salvation Army Headquarters in London. With the help of Wycliffe and one or two gifted musical friends she would fulfil some follow-up engagements which were still outstanding for the group, but the format and presentation would be quite different from that of the Joystrings.

Incidentally, on 1 April 1968 a press release was issued for all the national newspapers announcing that we were to disband and that our final performance would be given at the Fairfield Halls in Croydon on Friday 12 July. In some ways we had achieved what was thought to be our 'mission', which was to prove we could communicate the gospel in a modern pop idiom without getting caught up or dragged down in a medium often associated with glitz and glamour. In addition, all around the UK, and in some overseas countries too, Christian pop groups had sprung up, some copying our style and some developing their own, but all using modern lyrics and music to communicate the gospel. More than 200 groups were now operating within The Salvation Army in the UK alone, let alone in other churches. Joy's new task was to give oversight to these Salvationist pop groups throughout the country, to encourage and develop them – what an assignment!

For Peter and me, those couple of weeks after the end of the European tour were spent packing up our London home and moving to our new house in Wokingham. It is hard to believe that just two days before Bill's wedding in Bath, the Joystrings were singing once again in London at Westminster Central Hall. This time it was for Word in Action – a fund-raising event to provide Bibles for India and Sudan. The Rev Lord Soper was the speaker for the occasion and the organist, who played two marvellous organ voluntaries, was Dr W. S. Lloyd Webber, father of Lord Andrew Lloyd Webber and his cellist brother Julian! We were privileged to have two spots in the programme in which we could present our music.

Another interesting last engagement to tuck in was on 3 July when we were guests at another huge fund-raising event held at the Hilton Metropole hotel and conference centre in Brighton. It was a hair and fashion show, with the Joystrings presenting music for the evening and all proceeds going to Rehabilitation of the Disabled (REHAB). With Wycliffe's professional interest in designing buildings especially with the disabled in mind, we were more than happy to take part in this particular fund-raiser.

FAREWELL CONCERT

FRIDAY 12 July 1968 in the Fairfield Halls, Croydon, South London, was the venue for the Joystrings' final concert. It was filled to capacity with around 1,600 people, and the programme ran from 7.30pm to 10.30pm. It certainly wasn't the normal kind of concert we were used to giving – this was more or less a précis of the five years of Joystrings history, our raison d'être.

Beginning quietly with a song sung by Peter and Bill, 'Love That's in My Heart', we made a statement which was as true on that occasion as it had been when we commenced our special musical ministry. A prayer by Colonel Laurids Knutzen gave thanks for 'the faith, love and deportment of the Joystrings in places where men seldom hear God's name', after which the leader of The Salvation Army in Great Britain, Commissioner Will Cooper, gave his own words of appreciation for our ministry. Then it was the turn of our number one fan, Hazel Hunt, who had faithfully followed the group whenever possible to concerts and performances around the country, to speak her special words of thanks.

Eventually we were able to present some of our music: pieces carefully selected to portray memories or significant moments in the group's development and evangelistic outreach. Each one of us also spoke of the part we had played over the five years, and naturally we offered our own vote of thanks to those who

'Colonel Laurids Knutzen gave thanks for "the faith, love and deportment of the Joystrings in places where men seldom hear God's name"'

Above: Thoughtful moments on stage **Top right:** Bill and Jean

had helped our ministry – EMI and Abbey Road studios, the press, TV companies and of course our wonderful audiences everywhere we went. We also voiced special thanks to our Salvation Army leaders for the trust placed in us throughout the years and for the foresight in allowing it to happen at all.

Symbolic of the results of our ministry and a token of the effectiveness of our musical ministry was the introduction of the Davies family from Gloucester – seven of them – who all came to faith as a result of the Joystrings' music and message. Mrs Davies spoke from her heart on behalf of the whole family.

Naturally, as with all our concerts, after Joy had finally spoken her own words on the occasion, we sang some of the group's beautiful prayer songs in moments of dedication.

PALACE CAVALCADE

ALTHOUGH the Fairfield Halls evening had been billed as our final concert, we still had two more engagements scheduled before we bowed out. Both were connected to the fact that 1968 was promoted as The Salvation Army's Youth Year, with all kinds of activities and events geared towards young people. So it was natural that we were invited to a service especially for youth in the Westminster Central Hall, London, on the evening of Wednesday 24 July. It was a great celebratory occasion which included the Archdeacon of Westminster, Dr Edward Carpenter, General Frederick Coutts, who had been so instrumental in allowing the Joystrings to 'happen', and ourselves along with

Above: Farewell faithful fans!

other representative Salvation Army music groups. Together we provided a whole spectrum of Salvationist music for the young people who gathered.

Three days later, more than 50,000 people passed through the gates of Crystal Palace, South London, to enjoy what was billed as the 1968 Congress Cavalcade, featuring music, field displays, sports events and pageantry. Once again our international leader, General Coutts, was taking the salute, ably supported by the Chief of Staff, Commissioner Erik Wickberg, and the British Commissioner, Will Cooper. Commencing at 10.30am on a gloriously sunny day, the morning saw marching competitions between brass bands, festivals given by young people's choirs and programmes presented by overseas youth bands.

A Joystrings concert was the first main attraction after lunch,

set in a marquee which was filled to capacity with 3,000 young folk awaiting our absolutely final public appearance! Each member of the group (with the exception of our drummer Wycliffe) presented and sang at least one of their own compositions, and we ended the concert with the song which had soared into the charts when first performed – 'It's an Open Secret'. The audience were really on form, and cried out 'More, more!'

And so it was that we sang that final song again and again. The last glimpse those gathered had of any of us in our grey Joystrings uniforms was to see each of us carried high on the shoulders of hefty fans, to the flag mast a quarter of a mile away!

ON REFLECTION

IT'S now 50 years since the Joystrings came into being, and considering that we were only in existence for five years, the success and influence both in ministry and music achieved in that short time has remained. At the time we were disbanding, a gifted writer and officer-colleague, Captain Malcolm Bale, wrote the following:

The Salvation Army was built by men who had the imagination to experiment with new ideas, the faith to persist in them despite criticism, and the courage to discard them before they even began to die a natural death.

Some young hotheads like myself had begun to despair of the Army ever producing such men again. […]

But it happened! […] It was General Coutts who set the ball rolling when, in his first television interview on being elected, he spoke of talking to people in a language which they understood, and of approaching 'coffee-bar' young people with 'coffee-bar music'.

And whenever I've been tempted to think that the Joystrings had not been allowed to explore this new approach to the full, I've had to remind myself of the modern miracle that made even their continued existence possible: the sympathetic encouragement of leaders who were prepared to let youth talk to youth in a language youth could understand – even if their elders didn't!

But the question keeps on returning: were the Joystrings allowed to go far enough? Should there have been more 'Hippodrome' appearances and fewer concerts for middle-aged Salvationists? Would they have done much better had their tours of the country been arranged on a commercial basis, with one-night stands not in the local Army hall but in the clubs and pubs where young people already gather to hear beat groups?

One of the most commendable things about the Joystrings was the way in which, having been pushed into the pop world, they entered wholeheartedly into all that this involved without sacrificing or compromising their Salvationism. They were respected by other artists not simply because they were professionals, but because they had made themselves professionals for the sake of the gospel.

[…] Criticism, too […] has always been part of the price of pioneering.

Sometimes the Joystrings have failed miserably, usually because they were being used in the wrong place in the wrong way. They have been at their best when fulfilling the mission they believed to be almost uniquely theirs: making contact with the 'beat generation' in the cellar clubs and on the city streets, and challenging the 'beaten generation' in places like the Playboy and the Blue Angel.

[…] But good ideas, like good people, have a way of attaining immortality; and if the Joystrings, as a group, must die, it is in the confident expectation that the idea they personified will continue to grow and bear fruit.

This is the time for others to take their inheritance of musical technique, spiritual enthusiasm and public goodwill; and to better what has already been done. May God give them the gift of creative imagination, the wisdom to use it to the best advantage, and the courage gracefully to yield to a new generation of experimenters (for the gospel's sake) when their work is done!

The Vanguard, 8 August 1968, pp.20-21

'The last glimpse those gathered had of any of us in our grey Joystrings uniforms was to see each of us carried high on the shoulders of hefty fans, to the flag mast a quarter of a mile away!'

Right: Joy carried aloft by adoring fans
Far right: 'Our' General proudly looks on

Left: Joy, with Brenda, Lilian and Thelma

15

WHAT
HAPPENED
NEXT?

ONE OF THE QUESTIONS OFTEN ASKED is, 'What happened to the members of the group when the Joystrings disbanded?' The earlier part of this book mentions the changes of personnel which took place, some after the initial few months and others subsequently as required over the five years. I shall therefore mention here just those members who have contributed the most in length of time they were in the group and the musical contributions given over the years.

For various reasons, the three girls initially selected for the group – Brenda, Lilian and Thelma – all moved on from Salvation Army officership after a few years to pursue other careers. Handel Everett continued in Salvation Army appointments in the United Kingdom, giving more than 40 years of sterling service; and Lars Dunberg, although not continuing as an officer, has devoted himself to effective Christian ministry throughout the world.

JOY WEBB

ORDER OF THE FOUNDER (OF)

JOY'S grandfather had played in the Royal Sussex Staff Band in the British Army and had been a composer of military band music. Her father, as a boy, had been attracted to The Salvation Army by a drumming display in a Coventry market place, and this led to his becoming a Salvation Army officer. So it was not surprising that Joy, as a girl, soon became influenced not only with a love for the gospel and for music but also, stimulated by her father, for extraordinary instruments such as the phono-fiddle, the vibraphone and even the drums! Joy also became an accomplished pianist and songwriter and her music today is played and sung all around the world.

When Joy Webb entered the Salvation Army Training College in Denmark Hill, South London, her gifted piano playing and beautiful singing voice drew her to the attention of the training college staff. Shortly after she was commissioned as a full-time officer, Joy was called back to join the staff of the college, and among other duties, to take

responsibility for the women's singing brigade. It was the time when Joy, along with some cadets, was just beginning to experiment with guitars. It was therefore natural, when General Coutts made his chance remark to the press about the possibility of a Salvation Army pop group, that it would be to Joy Webb that the leaders would turn.

Joy's prolific songwriting for the group over those five years resulted in most of those songs being recorded. When the Joystrings ended she continued to fulfil some of the invitations which kept on pouring in, with a group of musicians who were available to her, some of them musician friends and colleagues known to her over the years. With her group known as the Joyfolk she successfully toured many countries, and more new songs emerged from this work. At the same time she was given responsibility for managing and encouraging the new Salvation Army pop groups which had sprung up all over the UK – a challenging task.

Later Joy went on to found the Marylebone Arts Centre in London, where she and her drama team encouraged young talent in the presentation of the gospel through dramatic art and music. At the same time she was training young singers and making recordings with the Sunbury Junior Singers, and appearing at all kinds of events in Britain and overseas. In later years she began writing books about her life, her work, her songwriting and her prayer life, and contributed to Salvation Army publications. She has also written and produced 15 musicals using and developing local aspiring artists and musicians. Joy has always believed, along with most artistes, that all art forms are intrinsically linked, from music to painting, to dance, to writing, to poetry and to theatre. She certainly deserved her Order of the Founder (the highest award for a member of The Salvation Army) for all her work with the arts.

In retirement Joy continues to write and has produced the most wonderful music and spiritual lyrics which are being used all around the world especially for choirs, and her music is often incorporated into brass band arrangements. In addition to all this she maintains a faithful membership at her local Salvation Army.

Above: Joy and her officer parents, Burnal and Irene Webb **Above right:** Joy, watched by her father, plays the vibraphone **Right:** Joy **Below:** Lars **Bottom:** Handel

Left: Joy receiving the Order of the Founder from the Commissioner (later Gerneral) Shaw Clifton **Below left:** Wycliffe and Liz **Below right:** Wycliffe, our exceptional drummer

WYCLIFFE NOBLE

OBE, FRIBA, FRSA

NOW honourably retired, Wycliffe was an architect by profession with his own practice specialising in design for the disabled. After qualifying as an architect he was invited to join the design team and staff as co-ordinating architect for the 1951 Festival of Britain's South Bank Exhibition. He has studied in Europe, Scandinavia, the United States, Canada and Japan, and in 1975 received the DoE Award for Wheelchair Housing. He was awarded the OBE in the New Year's Honours List of 1976. He has

117

served on numerous public committees developing access for disabled people, and latterly was Trustee Architect to ADAPT (Access for Disabled People to Arts Premises Today).

Some of his later achievements were to restore Park House on the Royal Sandringham Estate as a Country Park Hotel for disabled visitors, and to provide disabled access for the Royal Albert Hall. In November 2010 Wycliffe received the Person of the Year Award from RADAR – the Royal Association for Disability Rights.

He is married to Liz and they have two sons, Jan and Kim, both involved in the performing arts. Wycliffe gives wonderful credit to Liz, who is also the daughter of Salvation Army officers, for her great understanding in trying to balance her own career in teaching and motherhood with Wycliffe's frequent absence from his architectural practice in order to fulfil Joystrings engagements.

As with Joy, Peter, Bill and Pauline, Wycliffe's own parents were Salvation Army officers. He grew up within the ranks, moving about often as their appointments were changed. Among his earliest memories as a young lad was when they lived in Wick, in the north of Scotland. He would sit and watch the fishing boats on the Moray Firth and the ever-changing sounds of the North Sea were music to his ears. It was when Major and Mrs Charles Noble were appointed to Liverpool Kensington Salvation Army Corps that Wycliffe began to have piano lessons. At the same time he joined the young people's band and became quite adept on the side drum. In addition he learned to play the tubular bells, cornet, xylophone and piano accordion. He received his first certificate for pianoforte from London Trinity College of Music before he was eight years of age. His expertise in music appreciation and performance continued throughout his teens and into adulthood as Wycliffe became a senior bandsman in The Salvation Army.

Wycliffe's serious interest in drumming began with the timpani when he was tutored by Jack Wilson of the Royal Opera House, Covent Garden, and later in modern drumming by jazz master Kenny Clare of the famous Johnny Dankworth and Ted Heath Bands.

His ability to juggle his architectural practice, his home and family life and the amount of time he needed to commit to being the drummer in the Joystrings never ceased to amaze the rest of the group, either then or even now when we reflect on just how busy a schedule we ran over those five years. And he had time to talk to fans afterwards, sign autographs and help with packing up of equipment. Wycliffe has always been an incredibly calm person, full of wisdom and able to come up with an alternative suggestion when anything happened to upset the equilibrium of 'a day in the life of the group'.

BILL DAVIDSON

MDIV, DTH

OUR gifted lead guitarist with the fabulous tenor voice married his childhood sweetheart Jean in June 1968 when the Joystrings disbanded. They were appointed to The Salvation Army's work in Streatham Vale and Loughborough Junction in South London. During this time they had a daughter, Kellie, and a son, Craig. After two years serving in the Music Department of the Army's National Headquarters they went to Newark in Nottinghamshire, where they both confess to undergoing a huge spiritual change in their lives. During that time they felt that God wanted them to change their direction in Christian mission.

Bill and Jean entered Youth with a Mission (YWAM) in 1974, taking responsibility for the media department in the UK. They also directed several Discipleship Training Schools in Britain and Canada. These years of service with YWAM saw them minister throughout Europe, Scandinavia and the Middle East, behind the Iron Curtain, and throughout North and South America.

In 1978 the Davidsons visited Lake Luzerne in upstate New York for a series of meetings, during which Bill heard a call from God: 'This is your place. These are your people. This is home, to you!' In 1981 they migrated to the United States and founded Mountainside Christian Fellowship. Bill later changed the name to Church of the Nations (COTN), a name thereafter adopted by a number of related churches. Several churches were planted out of COTN – Lake Luzerne, including Abundant Life in Saratoga, NY; First Church of Granville, NY; Iglesia de Las Naciones, Los Olivos, Bogota, Colombia (now called Oasis Church); and La Esperanza children's home in Colombia. In 1983 Bill and Jean founded The King's School in Hadley, NY. Another child was added to their family in 1986 when John William was adopted out of Colombia. In 1995 Bill and Jean led a dozen members of COTN to yet another church plant, their present ministry at Church of The King in Queensbury, NY.

Bill travels extensively as a member of the Co-ordinating Team of Alliance International Ministries (AIM). This team of apostolic men has joined their lives and their ministries to serve churches and Christian leaders throughout the world. Bill and Jean regularly visit other churches in order to establish and encourage others in ministry and to help build their churches on biblical foundations, with a particular interest in the Northeast of the USA, Spain, South Asia, South America and West Africa. Both Bill and Jean are ordained into the ministry and Jean is a gifted administrator, leader and teacher in her own right while still supporting Bill's ministry. Bill has continued to study in order to develop his ministry.

Together their energies are also geared to giving oversight to the Esperanza Foundation which began when La Esperanza children's home in Colombia was founded by Jean 20 years ago. The work is now concentrated on the streets of Bogota at the Iglesia Oasis. Regular support is also given to the Liberian Christian Evangelical School System in Monrovia, the capital of Liberia, West Africa. Bill continues his music ministry by composing and recording songs for contemporary worship.

PETER AND SYLVIA (née GAIR) DALZIEL

AFTER the Joystrings disbanded in July 1968, Peter and I had responsibility for three Salvation Army corps in the UK – Wokingham, Aldershot and Chester-le-Street – before being transferred to the staff of the Salvation Army Training College in London. Within two years Peter was appointed as Youth Secretary in the Southampton and Channel Isles Division.

Above: Bill and Jean's wedding
Far left: Wycliffe
Left: Bill

During this time, while Peter was travelling, I concentrated on raising our two young sons, Emil and Marcel, while completing further university studies in theology and Church history with London University.

In 1978 we were transferred to South Africa. Peter was appointed as Territorial Youth Secretary for The Salvation Army in that region, and it was while we were in South Africa that we became involved in the development of media work – writing for and appearing in many religious and current affairs programmes on television. At one point we were hosting a Sunday half-hour guest programme on television. There followed a natural transition into public relations work with Peter as Public Relations Secretary and me as Public Relations Officer for the city of Johannesburg.

In 1982 we returned to the UK and were appointed to the corps and community of Croydon, followed by an appointment on The Salvation Army's International Headquarters (IHQ) to give oversight to a special training college development programme. We were then transferred to Sydney, Australia in 1986 in the Army's Public Relations Department there, where Peter had responsibility for directing and co-ordinating the bi-centennial celebrations. Leadership of the Salvation Army Music Department completed our four and a half years in Australia.

We returned to the UK in January 1991 so that our youngest son, Marcel, could begin his university course later that year. Our eldest son, Emil, also decided to return to England to pursue his own career. Peter was appointed Head of the Communications Resources Department at International HQ while I was made Director for The Salvation Army's Schools and Colleges Information Service for the United Kingdom. Four years later Peter became International Communications Secretary. During his term of office he undertook and completed further studies in operational business management. In June 1998 I took on the dual role of editor of an international women's magazine and Associate Training Officer, with particular responsibility for the training and development of International Headquarters personnel, and in 1999 Peter added to his responsibilities the role of Under Secretary for Resources at IHQ.

Finally, in October 2002 Peter was appointed Chief Secretary for the Netherlands and Czech Republic Territory, and I became Territorial Secretary for Women's Ministries for those countries.

Within the restraints of our official appointments as officers of The Salvation Army we have always taken every advantage for personal ministry and have been blessed with invitations to conduct services and seminars in the UK, Germany, Canada, the USA, South America, Australia and New Zealand, using our particular gifts of music and communication in concert. Having developed over the years as a 'musical duo' we have continued to make our own recordings – an obvious extension to our time spent with the Joystrings. We continue a very active life conducting services and leading weekends across the United Kingdom, along with some overseas ministry.

PAULINE (née JANE) BANKS

WITHIN weeks of her being married to Lieutenant Keith Banks, it was discovered that Pauline had serious health issues. Although she underwent several surgical procedures she was to be plagued with such issues for the rest of her life. As a consequence, Pauline had to leave the Joystrings in December 1965. Undeterred, she never allowed her condition to weaken her resolve to continue her life as an active officer in The Salvation Army. She used her own creative gifts to the full, complementing Keith's own abilities and ably fulfilling independent roles which followed. With Pauline's superb soprano voice and Keith's musical prowess on the piano and in music and lyrics composition, their relationship was obviously going to have music running through it for the duration.

Their nine years in corps appointments saw them working in Enfield, Crouch End, Skegness, Clapton and Carlisle. There followed two divisional appointments in charge of youth work in Nottingham and South London and a further four years in Scotland, with Keith's appointment as Territorial Youth Secretary and Pauline in her role as Territorial Guide Organiser. Together they then spent three years on the staff of The Salvation

Army's training college in London, with Keith as Senior Training Officer. Then came four years in the North London Division of The Salvation Army, with Pauline as Director of Women's Organisations and Keith as Divisional Commander.

Pauline and Keith had always wanted to work overseas, but Pauline's need to be close to good medical attention seemed to preclude this. However, in 1994 when an opportunity came for Keith and Pauline to head up the work in Papua New Guinea, they decided to risk all and, despite the tropical conditions in which they would be working, felt it was a right decision. The four years they spent there needed every ounce of courage and determination they could find, but it was a truly rewarding experience for them both.

In 1998, after a few weeks of homeland furlough in England, Pauline and Keith were appointed to Japan, Keith as Chief Secretary and Pauline as Secretary for Women's Organisations in that country. However, towards the end of 1999 Pauline became very ill, and cancer of the ileum was diagnosed. Surgery and chemotherapy followed until the couple were transferred back to England. For several years Pauline struggled to regain strength and keep the cancer at bay. She still undertook a role on International Headquarters in London as International Statistician and assistant secretary to several boards, while Keith was Secretary for International Personnel.

Pauline's cancer remission was short-lived, for in 2004 she was diagnosed with two brain tumours and had to undergo surgery once again. It was about this time that they decided to make the move to West Scotland in readiness for their retirement and to be close to their daughter, Alison, and her family. Their son, Craig, lives in Los Angeles. Keith – and Pauline when she was well enough – continued their work as officers by representing the head of the UK Salvation Army in Scotland. Sadly, just over a year later Pauline lost her sight and the tumours began to grow again. She was very ill when, with Keith, they celebrated their life of service as Salvation Army officers in December 2007 and officially retired.

Before Pauline passed away in 2009, she fulfilled a life-long dream of hers – to make a personal CD with her singing

'Having developed over the years as a "musical duo" we have continued to make our own recordings – an obvious extension to our time spent with the Joystrings'

Top: Sylvia and Peter **Above left:** Pauline **Above:** At the London Transport Museum

Keith's songs and Keith reading some of his poetry. *The Greatest Adventure* is a celebration of these wonderful gifts.

RUTH (née SWAINSBURY) HOWES

WHEN after singing for a year with the Joystrings Ruth married Lieutenant Cliff Howes, they were appointed to Salvation Army work in South Wales. But life for Ruth and Cliff underwent a massive change while they were the officers in charge of The Salvation Army in Aberfan. On 21 October 1966 a waste tip of slag slid down a mountainside into the mining village below, engulfing Pantglas Junior School and 20 houses. In total 144 people died, 116 of them schoolchildren. Ruth had just given birth to their first child, their daughter, but she and Cliff were deeply involved for months trying to help people through the awful trauma of losing so many friends and loved ones. After a while they found themselves at a stage of total 'burn-out' and felt the need to resign from the relentless pressures of that particular role.

They set up home in Harlow, Essex, where Cliff had previously been in charge of the Salvation Army church, and Cliff began training in the Probation Service, eventually becoming a senior probation officer. With two children to look after by this time, Ruth took on part-time secretarial work and as the children grew she became PA to a marketing executive.

The aftermath of the Aberfan disaster haunted them constantly and it took them both many years to fully work through this trauma. But for recreation the family joined the local canoe club. This simple activity gradually brought some degree of healing to their lives at a time when their personal Christian faith had been sorely challenged. When, after surgery, Ruth could no longer lift her canoe, she moved on to bowling and discovered a natural aptitude for the game, since not only did she end up playing for Essex but took up umpiring the game as well. This led to Ruth umpiring at the Commonwealth Games in Manchester and at two World Bowls, one in England and one in New Zealand. She became President of England Bowls and was asked to stand for election as a Director of Bowls England. Her training as a Salvation Army officer in public speaking and communication stood her in good stead for when she was Vice Chair of Bowls England.

Ruth also spent five years on the Harlow Bench as a magistrate, using her former experience as a Salvation Army officer in caring for and dealing fairly with people, to help her in her decisions.

In the last few years Ruth and Cliff have 'returned' to their Salvation Army roots and redefined their Christian values and beliefs. This was actually through an amazing sequence of events, but events which in Ruth's own words definitely add up to them being led by a force outside of themselves.

NIGEL ROBSON

NIGEL joined the Joystrings in May 1966 as a young lad who had only recently left school. He was at the time playing lead guitar in a local Salvation Army group called The Persuaders, but he was also a talented keyboard player and had a wonderful tenor voice. The opening for him to join the Joystrings arose when Peter and I became engaged and I felt I needed a few months away from group life.

Before joining the Joystrings Nigel had already written about his awakening to the music of J. S. Bach and the influence that this composer had on his life. Little did he realise at the time just how important this awakening was to be on his life when he eventually moved on from the Joystrings. In May 1967 Nigel returned to study and to his real love – classical music. He became one of Britain's leading lyric tenors, known for his baroque and 20th-century operatic repertory, especially the music of Benjamin Britten. He studied with Alexander Young and Gustave Sacher, and has performed at British, European, and Japanese music festivals. His warm, flexible voice has been ideal for the many works Britten wrote for Sir Peter Pears.

Nigel has performed at the Welsh National Opera, Lisbon Opera, Opera North, the Grand Theatre of Tours, Glyndebourne, the Edinburgh Festival, the Almeida Opera Festival, the *Orchestre National de Lille* (where he sang in Bach's *St John Passion*), St Petersburg, Prague, Tel Aviv, Amsterdam,

Paris, Milan and Rotterdam as well as making many concert appearances. In addition, he has worked with leading period instrument ensembles including The Orchestra of the Age of Enlightenment, and with other ensembles specialising in new music such as Ensemble Modern. One has to wonder what that brief interlude of singing, touring and recording with the Joystrings had on Nigel's overall musical journey!

Nigel is married to opera director Olivia Fuchs, and they live in London with their children Lucas and Carlotta.

NUMBER ONE FAN

HAZEL Hunt was just one of many thousands of young people whose lives were influenced and changed because of the music and ministry of the Joystrings. But there is a special reason for mentioning Hazel in this book. She was, without doubt, our number one fan, utterly devoted and almost fanatical about being present, whenever time and money allowed, at our concerts and performances. Occasionally in press photographs Hazel pops up somewhere in the background! Photographing and collecting media cuttings about the group were paramount to her over the years the group was in existence. Indeed, a great deal of the chronological information we have in this book must be attributed to Hazel's diligence in collecting material.

Since Hazel was just 17 when the group decided to disband, she was very young when she first came under the influence of the Joystrings. She confesses to having attended around 90 concerts and having travelled more than 3,500 miles to get to them! At one point she even was ready to book her holiday in Malta so that she could be present for the Joystrings' visit there, but a political upheaval in the country at the time caused the group's visit to the island to be cancelled. It was a tribute to her absolute dedication that she was asked to speak at our farewell concert at the Fairfield Halls in July 1968 – and she did a wonderful job!

Hazel has continued throughout the years to be a Salvationist. Married to Rob Shackleton, they have three grown-up children – Aay-Jay, Edward and Stuart – and they live in Winchester.

Above: Together with Pauline at Trafalgar Square

'It was a tribute to Hazel's absolute dedication that she was asked to speak at our farewell concert at the Fairfield Halls in July 1968 – and she did a wonderful job!'

From below left: Hazel Hunt; Hazel and Peter; Nigel; Ruth

16

FAR-REACHING INFLUENCE

PERSONAL REFLECTIONS

I DON'T remember hearing much music in my home, certainly not as a small child. Growing up on the Northumbrian coast, my early interests lay in sand lizards, shells, windswept sand dunes and reading – oh, how I loved reading! Later on my interests stretched to farm animals, since a change of home found us living next to a farm. There I learned to milk a cow by hand, churn butter, feed the livestock and collect the eggs. Nothing could give me greater pleasure in those years of childhood than being involved with animals – except perhaps going to school. I had a natural aptitude for learning, as my senior years at school would prove. However, subconsciously, the little music I was exposed to must have been making an impact somewhere upon my heart and mind because, to this day, I remember clearly the words of a beautiful song which we sang in junior school assembly – a song which has come to mean so much and echoes the sentiments of all that my life has become over the years:

> *God make my life a little light*
> *Within the world to glow;*
> *A little flame that burneth bright,*
> *Wherever I may go.*
> *God make my life a little flower*
> *That giveth joy to all,*
> *Content to bloom in native bower,*
> *Although the place be small.*
> *God make my life a little song*
> *That comforteth the sad,*
> *That helpeth others to be strong,*
> *And makes the singer glad.*
> *God make my life a little staff*
> *Whereon the weak may rest,*
> *That so what health and strength I have*
> *May serve my neighbours best.*

(Matilda Betham-Edwards)

In preparation for my move to a girls' school in the city of Durham, my family made another house move, and it was then that I discovered The Salvation Army. One Sunday, walking through the village, West Rainton, I heard music and walked towards the sound. The door of a small wooden building stood open, and as I drew nearer I could see that inside there was a display of fruits, vegetables and sheaves of corn. It was September; it was the time of Harvest Festival. Of course I knew all about that, having been involved in harvesting on the farm, but it was the music of thanksgiving which attracted me to the building. The rest is history, as the saying goes. For the first time in my life, apart from school assemblies, I came under the influence of religious music, for I joined this little Salvation Army church, becoming a member of the junior choir and learning to play a brass instrument.

My new school in the city also provided more classical teaching in music appreciation. I could have learned the violin or the flute but did not feel inclined to either. Instead, using my voice was something else. I discovered I loved singing and would often be invited to be the girl soloist at the neighbouring boys' senior school when they did their end of year musical. In the late 1950s skiffle was having its short-lived fling, and when some of the senior schoolboys decided to form a skiffle group they would often ask me to sing with them. Music for me was fun and it was a means by which a very shy girl from the country could have a sense of identity.

However, it was only when I went to the Salvation Army training college in London in August 1963 that music and singing became more than just fun. Suddenly the words I was singing became much more important – I discovered that music was far-reaching and could be a real means of communication. As a member of the female choir in college, the 'singing brigade', under the leadership and tuition of Captain Joy Webb, I discovered there was no emotion or feeling which a piece of music could not communicate. This was certainly a spiritually awakening time for me, but opportunities to use this newly discovered gift emerged so fast they terrified me!

When we became Salvation Army officer cadets, none of us

who became involved in the Joystrings had any idea what was about to happen to us. In the quiet solitude of my own small student room I would often question what was happening to me. None of this was in my plans when I became a cadet.

The Old Testament reveals similar times of searching and questioning for the prophet Amos. He was a shepherd, a young man from the country upon whom God laid his hand and instructed to be his spokesperson, his communicator. The book that bears Amos's name tells that when he is challenged he states very clearly: 'I am no prophet nor a prophet's son; but I am a herdsman, and a dresser of sycamore trees, and the Lord took me from following the flock, and the Lord said to me, "Go, prophesy…"' (Amos 7:14–15, *Revised Standard Version*).

Throughout the years, music and singing has continued to be very much a part of my personal Christian ministry. And it is part of our united ministry, for Peter and I continue to work very closely together. Songs and music remind us of special people and significant occasions – music evokes memory. Of course in those days of the Joystrings we learned very quickly about the importance of presentation and communication, learning to think on one's feet and making quick adaptations. The years of experience in leadership have also served to give me confidence in public, but I think I shall always remain a shy soloist because, to a degree, that demands a projection of oneself, and I am still not at ease with that. In order to sing in public I have to remind myself constantly of the reason why I sing. I take strength from Psalm 63:7 – 'because you are my help, O Lord, I sing in the shadow of your wings'. Here for me is a promise of continued strength and divine protection and guidance under the wings of the Divine Eagle who shadows my every move. The first verse of Psalm 45 finds an echo in my personal prayer:

May my heart be stirred by a noble theme as I recite verses for my King: may my tongue be as the pen of a skilful writer and my lips anointed with grace. Then my life will not only be in song, but my whole life will become a song.

Throughout the years the group members have met countless people who confess to being influenced by the message and music of the Joystrings and I am most grateful that a few of them have agreed to share with the world their own personal story.

MAJOR NIGEL BOVEY
ASSISTANT EDITOR IN CHIEF THQ AND EDITOR OF THE WAR CRY

THE Sixties – I remember them. I was there. I was caught between two worlds. One was inhabited by Radio Luxembourg and the Beatles. The other revolved around my crest-emblazoned scarlet jersey and brass band learners' practice. Even as I was mastering the fingering on my grandfather's old cornet, my heart was set on getting my hands on a red electric guitar, like Hank Marvin's. Or, for that matter, any guitar.

As a lad, I had no lofty thoughts of using a guitar to praise God. Why would I? Foremost in Salvation Army music-making in my home corps of Exeter Temple was the band. The music that surrounded me on a Sunday was a world away from the music that was setting the world alight. Then I saw and heard the Joystrings!

One thousand people packed the hall to capacity the night the Joystrings came to town. I watched from the gallery – middle, front row. They had everything – Vox amps, just like the Beatles, Hofner violin bass, just like Paul McCartney, and a Rickenbacker electric guitar, just like John Lennon. Sorry, girls, I didn't notice you! (Some years later when Bill Davidson returned with his group Good News, they gigged in a local youth centre, with me on the Rickenbacker. God is good!)

I also remember seeing people over-fill the mercy seat that night. Although I never left my seat, a seed was sown – God's OK with the guitar.

The next time I saw the Joystrings was at Crystal Palace in London. It was the group's last appearance. They drove off into the sunset in a sports car. This was the end of an era. I leave others to judge the wisdom of that decision, but one consequence was that Joy was tasked with encouraging the use of 'rhythm groups' – oh, how we kids hated that name, still do! – across the territory. So instead of there being just one Salvation Army group, there would be many. One rocked up in Exeter.

I wanted in on the action. I traded my first camera for my first guitar. It took a while for the older kids to let me into the group. Then, having religiously learned the chords of the Joystrings' songs (it was a genius idea to publish that music – the first Army guitar song books?), I was allowed to 'sing it and shout it' with the rest of them. Ever since, the guitar has been an integral part of my mission, songwriting and leading of worship.

God's river of grace has many tributaries. It was while I was conducting a student Bible study that he called me to spiritual leadership. But I am convinced that without the message of the Joystrings – not a song but their existence – I would not have been a Salvation Army officer for the past 30-plus years.

The Joystrings changed the face and sound of church music. They dragged Christianity kicking and screaming into the new-born pop world. They connected with kids to whom God was dead. They struck a chord with one kid who was trying to make sense of two worlds: a kid who, as Editor of *The War Cry*, now goes and does likewise.

MAJOR GEORGE SCOTT
MAIDSTONE, KENT, UK

AT the beginning of the Sixties I had completed my engineering studies at Leeds University and had embarked upon my career in electrical engineering. I had crossed the Pennines and joined a company called Ferranti, but was seconded to the electrical engineering department of Manchester University where the Atlas computer, the first transistorised computer, was being developed. Towards the end of the project I moved south to a small company in Feltham that developed magnetic recording heads. To use a cliché, this was the cutting edge of technology. The British Aircraft Corporation was building the ill-fated TSR2 supersonic strike and reconnaissance aircraft which was eventually scrapped in 1965, and we were developing a 32-track system for one-inch recording tape for the plane. In engineering detail, the recording head needed 63 slots in the one-inch block of brass – 32 for the number of tracks and 31 for mu-metal screens to reduce crosstalk.

During this time I lived with my sister and her husband at Reading and commuted to Feltham daily. I worshipped with them at the Reading Central Corps of The Salvation Army and soon became involved in the various activities of the corps, playing in the band and singing in the songsters. I was then asked to lead the weekly Bible study for young people, then called corps cadets, which obviously involved an evening of preparation. Just to complete the week, I was also secretary for the London branch of the Salvation Army Students Fellowship, which met monthly but obviously required time to organise challenging speakers for the students and young graduates.

I still managed to find time for rugby in the winter and cricket in the summer. However, this busy schedule made it difficult for me to pursue my personal vision for the worshipping community of which I was part. I felt that I should be more involved outside the church serving the needs of the less fortunate. A lady who was handicapped was brought to my attention. She had just moved into a new house. The building site outside her house, euphemistically known as a garden, needed attention and the only time I had for this was Saturday mornings, sandwiched between my church activities and sport.

Thus was my life when the Joystrings visited Reading in their summer tour of 1964. Many of the songs they sang that night I had heard on radio, TV and on 45rpm vinyl discs. However, on that evening Peter Dalziel and Bill Davidson sang a new poignant number entitled 'The Ballad of a Good Man'. Two or three verses of the song described Jesus ministering to the needs of less fortunate people. The last verse told how the hands of Jesus which had met the needs of the disadvantaged were nailed to a cross.

The words of this song strongly challenged me. Was I prepared to pay a price for my vision – which was that I, through the Church, should be ministering to the needs of the marginalised as Jesus had done? Was I prepared to give up my life of engineering and sport so that I could serve others, and encourage others to do likewise? The obvious way to do this within The Salvation Army where I worshipped was to become an officer, which would present me with the leadership of a worshipping community but also give me the opportunity of serving within a local community.

That evening, along with others who were present, I said yes to that call from God which came through the ministry of the Joystrings. A year later I entered the Salvation Army Training College at Denmark Hill, London, to begin my training for a life of service, following in the footsteps of the Joystrings, most of whom had prepared to serve God in that same place.

Looking back over my 40 plus years as an officer, 20 of which have been spent in ministering to the underprivileged in India, I have to thank God for the rich quality of life that was mine, and to thank the Joystrings for being the instrument through which God spoke to me.

DR JANETTE DAVIES
INTERNATIONAL GENDER STUDIES AND INSTITUTE OF SOCIAL AND CULTURAL ANTHROPOLOGY, UNIVERSITY OF OXFORD, UK

IT was the Sixties and the family was living in Gloucester. We had lived in Singapore in the early part of the decade and had worshipped at a vibrant Anglican church there. However, on our return to the UK my father could not find a suitable church where he felt comfortable, until mother was offered family tickets for a Joystrings concert in Northgate Methodist Church.

'We were overwhelmed by the friendly welcome we were given and impressed with lively young people of our age, whose music spoke to the present age. From that Sunday on our lives revolved around The Salvation Army'

The music and the lyrics reflected the sounds of the era and I sensed a new approach to faith and belief in these songs. The instrumentals and vocal harmonies spoke to my Welsh soul, striking a personal chord that could only have been the voice of God. I was not the only one in our family to hear the voice of God that night, for as we watched and listened to the Joystrings, Dad responded to an appeal to pray.

It was during the concert that I became aware of my own sacred space and the hallowed prompting of God on my future. My career plans upon leaving school included training as a nurse, but I had not dwelt on it until the night of the concert. Formulating in my mind was a distinct thought, a question even – could I nurse for The Salvation Army anywhere in the world? I was completely unaware at that time of the Army's world-wide ministry, but as I opened my heart to the leadings of God, I had a definitive sense of calling – to nursing, yes, but now a calling which was encapsulated in The Salvation Army, new to me and new to the family.

The Sunday after the Joystrings concert proved to be a new dawn for us all. Dad accepted an invitation for the family to worship at Gloucester Corps – imagine, seven of us taking up a whole row of seats! We were overwhelmed by the friendly welcome we were given and impressed with lively young people of our age, whose music spoke to the present age. From that

'I had to choose between my covenant to God and the Army, and the man I loved. But it is amazing how God's hand was even in this'

Sunday on our lives revolved around The Salvation Army.

So what was the answer to my question as to whether I could nurse with The Salvation Army? Well, after training as a nurse and then as a Salvation Army officer, I was appointed to Cochabamba in Bolivia to commence the Army's medical work and open a clinic in a shanty town, which was followed by the opening of the Hospital Harry Williams. This was a fascinating era in a country under military dictatorship, so I learned fast what it takes to depend absolutely on God even for practical tasks such as stitching a wound for the first time. One of my scariest moments was planning the safe delivery of a baby for a woman who'd had 15 previous pregnancies. Subsequently I was appointed as officer/midwife on the Thai/Cambodian border as the Cambodian war was coming to an end. I was one of just two midwives attending 900 births in three months!

Following my time there I was appointed to the Army's extensive medical programme in Bangladesh. Two years into my appointment I met Jeff, a geologist working on a British government groundwater project. At that time there was a strict rule that Salvation Army officers could only marry officers. (Thankfully, that rule no longer applies.) This was the hardest moment of my life. I had to choose between my covenant to God and the Army, and the man I loved. But it is amazing how God's hand was even in this. Sadly I resigned my officership, but Jeff and I married and thus began a new future together. After two years of working in Fiji we came home to Oxford and I completed degrees in medical and social anthropology and then a doctorate in anthropology and ageing, studying cultures, people and societies. My experience as a Salvation Army officer

in developing countries continues to enable me in my academic life, such as carrying out research in Tanzania, Sri Lanka, Bangladesh and Georgia. The highlight was being asked to evaluate the HIV/Aids programme in Zambia. This showed me that my experience as a Salvation Army officer and my academic gifts and intellect could be combined usefully at The Salvation Army's Chikankata Mission Hospital. Only God's perfect timing could have made this possible.

My current research at the University of Oxford involves looking at ageing, and I believe that the insight and compassion needed as an officer continually complements the intellectual nature of all I do. Reflecting on the impact of the Joystrings on my teenage years, I acknowledge the profound effect of the whispered call of God heard in the music and lyrics during their concert. My response and subsequent beliefs have enabled me to become what God intended for me – his disciple both in The Salvation Army and the wider world. How different my life may have been without the ministry of the Joystrings!

LIEUT-COLONEL BILL HEELEY
DIVISIONAL COMMANDER, YORKSHIRE DIVISION, UK

I AM a Salvation Army officer today partly because of the music and influence of the Joystrings. When they emerged in the swinging Sixties, I was a teenager following a career path in a solicitors' practice in Liverpool. This was a decade that saw an explosion in music and fashion and when the voice of youth was heard across the world. 'Beatlemania' gripped the country, man landed on the moon, England won the football World Cup, parking meters were introduced, and sit-ins, love-ins, civil rights and flower power were the norm. Miniskirts and hot pants were all the fashion – all you needed was love!

The Sixties gave so much to the world, and much of it, certainly on the music scene, emanated from Merseyside, especially Liverpool. The city was awash with a plethora of pop groups aspiring to make it big time. Many of the local groups were discovered by agents and record companies in the clubs of Liverpool; the Cavern, located in the cellar of the offices in which I worked, was the most famous of them. The clubs, bands, trendsetting fashions, world-class architecture and thriving economy, all came together to make Liverpool the success story of the Sixties. You had to *be* there to truly know what it was like.

As a young Salvationist it was a real temptation for me to go the clubs to hear bands destined to become world-famous. However, just at the right time – God's time – the Joystrings burst on to the music scene to impact Salvationist youth in a way that no other Christian music group has done over the past 50 years, to my knowledge. The Joystrings became trendsetters for many young Salvationists. The expressed hope of General Frederick Coutts that The Salvation Army might show a modern approach in communicating the Christian gospel to the man in the street became a reality as, across the United Kingdom, without any encouragement other than the Holy Spirit's leading and the example set by the Joystrings, young people formed their own rhythm groups in an effort to communicate the gospel in a relevant way.

We bought cheap acoustic guitars and books claiming to make us Play the Guitar in a Day; we taught ourselves basic guitar chords – C, G, F, D7 and E minor – added a bass drum borrowed from the senior band and a side drum and cymbal bought on weekly payments from Kay's catalogue, and hey presto! we had a rhythm group.

The Victors was the rhythm group formed at my home corps of Rock Ferry, and it first appeared on stage at the Over-60s club! As we improved we extended our ministry to similar clubs in other corps and churches before being invited to appear at 'Through till Two', an event that provided a meeting place for Salvation Army young people at the Liverpool Congress Hall. From there, as our repertoire of songs and musical competency increased, we moved on to Christian youth clubs which in the Sixties attracted non-Christian young people in great numbers. The secular cellar clubs were no longer an attraction for me and my mates, as we were too busy rehearsing and playing music for our evangelistic concerts. We became more confident with public speaking too – we had to, because as we grew in confidence, we were invited to lead worship meetings. We had found a fulfilling ministry, and for me at least this proved to be a good training ground in preparation for my life's work as a Salvation Army officer.

As a result of attending Joystrings concerts, we learned from observation how to use songs as 'atmosphere builders', how to hold the attention of our audience, the importance of choosing the right song and the right moment to launch our relevant message to those present.

The Joystrings were not only trendsetters however, but role models. The Lord replaced the secular icons of the Liverpool music scene with positive Salvation Army officer role models, in particular the newly commissioned Lieutenants Peter Dalziel, Sylvia Gair and Bill Davidson. This was not some misplaced hero worship which drew me into officership for the wrong reasons, because the Lord had already called me to be an officer – I knew that. This was the simply the example of young officers straight out of training college with the love of the Lord in their hearts, taking risks for the sake of the gospel. They were radical, 'on the edge' on occasions. If *they* were willing to give their lives to the 'Long Lost Cause', to use the title of one of their songs, I wanted to be in there fighting alongside them! I thank God for the example and inspiration of the Joystrings whose ministry reached not only to the man in the street but also to young and not so young people in the Army.

Of all their songs, the words of one will forever be synonymous with my call to officership. Its message challenged me and resulted in the dedication of my life to God and The Salvation Army:

> You dream a long, long time of wealth and fame,
> A thousand easy ways to make your name.
> But in your heart you know it's not for you,
> For God is calling you his work to do.
> One life to live for him, and him alone,
> One love to give to him and all your own;
> A chance to spend your life on something true;
> All that is God's to give is here for you.

17

JOY
HAS
THE
LAST
WORD

THE JOYSTRINGS

IN 2011, REVIEWING THE DIGITALLY re-mastered *Joystrings Restrung* CD, Major Bruce Tulloch wrote in *Salvationist* magazine as follows: 'These tracks marked a revolution in ministry, one that arguably changed Salvation Army music and perhaps all of Christian music in the United Kingdom for ever.'

As I read these words my mind went back to the moment in 1965 when I opened a letter from the then Training Principal of our International Training College, Commissioner Clarence Wiseman, which simply said:

8 March 1965

My dear Captain,

THE JOYSTRINGS

I thought in all fairness I should let you see the Chief of Staff's reply to my letter in which I suggested the Joystrings should be continued for another full year at least.

It would appear from this letter that the plan to disband the group, when the centenary celebrations conclude, is to be carried out.

From now until then we do pray that the Lord will continue to honour your ministry.

Yours sincerely

Clarence D. Wiseman
Training Principal

PS. Kindly return the Chief's letter

It may surprise a lot of people to know that from the first days of the life of the Joystrings in November 1963, the group had existed completely under the direction of International Headquarters (IHQ) because, of course, we came to birth out of the *International* William Booth Memorial Training College (to give its full title as it was then). Our Training Principal had to refer every proposal and every invitation for this new group to the office of the Chief of Staff at IHQ. The answer, in many cases, would only come when General Frederick Coutts had himself considered the wisdom of our involvement in whatever project had been suggested. So then you will not be surprised that when I opened that letter… my heart sank! I knew deep within myself that the work the Holy Spirit had started through this Salvation Army pop group – as traumatic and spectacular as it had been over nearly two years – was by no means finished! I then did what I had always done – I laid the letter down in front of me and simply said: 'Lord, please show me what to do!'

In such moments as this one during the lifespan of the group, letters and phone calls of support and prayer promise would come into my mind and help me to pick myself up and sort through the problem more calmly. One such letter I have before me as I write this final chapter. It comes from none other than Catherine Bramwell Booth, granddaughter of the Founder of The Salvation Army. She writes:

You stand in a place of immense opportunity, which must, at times, seem a burden too heavy to bear. But you are His who called you – Jesus, our Saviour, whose word is to you when He says, 'I will not leave you'. Every now and then I pray for you, that the beloved Spirit of Jesus may companion you, speaking through you – His word of power to so many young hearts.
Praising God for you,
Your old comrade in the Army,
Catherine Bramwell Booth

As I began to think through the problem I realised what had triggered this instruction from the Chief of the Staff. The young cadets I had selected to be in the group would be ordained and commissioned as officers very shortly and as such would be expected to take up their life's work immediately in the United Kingdom. After all, the same thing had happened with my first three Joystrings girls nine months earlier. Why, then, did I feel it so wrong this time round? 'You have to do something' was ringing in my mind again and again. Yes, but what?

Little did I know that God the Holy Spirit was again right ahead of me, and whilst I was putting off telling the group of the Chief's decision to disband and writing desperate letters to anyone I thought might help, he was preparing the way forward for us.

The answer came through a wonderful visionary Salvation Army officer who, as head of the Army's work in the United Kingdom would have the pleasure of receiving these newly commissioned officers into his territory at the end of summer 1965 – the provisional time set for the group's demise. His name: Commissioner Will Cooper… of ever-blessed memory to anyone who knew him! I think we all knew he was a bit of a holy 'maverick', so I guess it was no surprise when we heard that he had announced that nobody was going to tell him what to do with his new young officers! Of course the Joystrings would not disband! The Army and the churches of Great Britain needed their ministry – to say nothing of the youngsters of the 'beat generation' – and he was going to see that need well met! Incidentally I don't know to this day how he managed to secure my transfer from the staff of the International Training College to what was then called the British Territory. However, transferred I was. Following that memorable Salvation Army Centenary summer we had a short break, after which the Joystrings came under Will Cooper's jurisdiction.

He gifted us with the love, guidance and support of the head of The Salvation Army's UK Music Department, Major Dean Goffin – later Commissioner Sir Dean Goffin. Commissioner Will Cooper and Major Dean Goffin were pivotal in saving the group for its future life and we would not have survived without their total embracing of the Holy Spirit's mission for us and their forward thinking of what we could be as an example for all young Christians in Great Britain in the 'swinging Sixties'. Without their continuing vision and support we would never have accomplished half the things you read about in this book

– our hugely popular television shows such as *Song Break*; our performances on *Songs of Praise*; our tours; concerts including benefit concerts like the one for the Aberfan disaster at the Royal Albert Hall – we were the only Christian content in that entire evening! But for their support we may never have continued writing and recording, and many of the beautiful meaningful songs we wrote in the last three years of our existence would never have been born! But for their belief in us we would never have taken this new idea in Christian communication to France, the Netherlands, Norway, Sweden, Belgium or anywhere else for that matter, and I salute these two remarkable officers who had the imagination and insight to set us free.

It would be easy to allow history to record universal support for us, our music and our mission. Of course, with hindsight it was only to be expected that some would miss the point of it entirely, but I would be less than honest if I did not say how debilitating it was for us sometimes to encounter vitriolic words from those who simply could not tolerate a change that was happening before their very eyes. I have learned over the years that change can be a dividing thing; often people react against it not because they see it as basically wrong but because they see it as a threat to the status quo they have enjoyed for so long. This panic reaction is increased when change appears to threaten their personal position or possibilities. One learns to deal with this kind of thing courteously, and hopefully with love, but when one is young, desperately tired (as we often were) and facing challenges never before imagined, it can almost defeat you.

I recall times at the beginning of the Joystrings' ministry when this was so. Only the overwhelming sense of presence of the Holy Spirit kept us going. To me, it was so surprising that reassurance often came to us from people who I felt were not particularly associated with religion. Like, for example, theatre actor and director Sir Bernard Miles who wrote to me:

> I've never particularly liked Christians until I worked with the Joystrings.

This he stated after we had done several performances with

his company at the Mermaid Theatre in Queen Victoria Street, very near to The Salvation Army's International Headquarters.

I should also record how many times, when faced with disapproval for what we were attempting to do and be, we found comfort and strength in remembering our Founder, William Booth. It is impossible to count the times we said to one another, 'The Founder would do this!' or 'The Founder would understand this!' Sometimes we had a strong sense that he was with us, urging his young pioneers on and ever on. Oh, we so hoped we would not fail him or our Lord in all our endeavours!

Of course we were fully aware of the persecution suffered by the first Salvationists in the 19th century. But nothing prepared Pauline and me for being spat on during the great Crystal Palace day in the summer of 1965 during the Army's Centenary celebrations, or indeed when we received the news that a church in Redruth where we had recently given a concert had been re-consecrated by the bishop before the congregation were allowed back in to worship. How the devil must have rejoiced that day!

I suppose the most serious objections to our ministry came during the 'For God's Sake Care' campaign of the Army – that massive fundraising appeal for £3 million for our social work development. Proposed by the Army's Public Relations Department, the suggestion was to have the Playboy bunny girls sell £1 bonds on the streets of London for the appeal. Sylvia has told the story of how the answer from the Playboy Club was a resounding 'yes' – but only if they could have the Joystrings sing in the club for three successive nights! I must confess we in the group were more than amazed that the Public Relations personnel accepted the deal on our behalf – we had no choice in the matter! And it goes without saying that we were more than a little apprehensive.

Somehow publicity photos showing Peter and me with a bunny girl appeared in most national newspapers, and shots of us performing in the Playboy Club were shown on the TV news both in the UK and in the USA the night we started, with the bunny girls dancing on the disco floor front of us. No mention was made that we had in fact complained that we were not happy with being on the disco floor part of the club where no one really listened to our music, or indeed that we had on the second and third nights moved up to the cabaret floor where our message in song was actually listened to.

I recall we went on stage about 1.30am and were received very generously indeed – which is a great help when one's eyelids are closing and a firm grasp on the lyrics of songs seems to be quickly evaporating. I thanked God that at least by now we could write songs competently, with lyrics that would challenge and demand a more thoughtful response. But of course we were in an environment that none of us had ever experienced, and quite honestly would have preferred not to have experienced. It was certainly a challenging environment for our young men, but perhaps even more so for Sylvia and me when we girls discovered that we were sharing a dressing room with the bunny girls who, with carefree abandonment, stripped off their tight-bodiced bunny suits to cool down. However, after the first shock to our systems we did eventually get to know one or two of them – young mothers and all!

I arrived home to my flat in East Dulwich, South London, from the Playboy Club at 4.30am absolutely exhausted, and crawled into bed around 5am. I was awakened by a call shortly before 8am advising me that the General wished to see me as soon as I could make it to IHQ. I haven't words to describe how I felt after just a couple of hours' rest, but I dressed in my uniform and made my way by public transport to 101 Queen Victoria Street. What on earth had we done now?

I guess the doorman of IHQ must have been surprised to see me, as it was well known that the Joystrings had spent the early hours of the morning in the Playboy Club. But he made the call to the General's office to announce my arrival. The General's secretary came out to meet me and announced, 'The General will see you now, Captain!' General Frederick Coutts sat behind his desk, and standing next to him was Commissioner Erik Wickberg, Chief of the Staff, whom I had never seen before. 'Please sit down, Captain,' said the General. I sat! Leaning towards me, the General said to me in his deep sonorous tones,

'Captain, I want to ask you – do you feel you ought to be at the Playboy Club?'

Oh no! I thought, that's the wrong question!

'Sir,' I said, 'if you had asked me if we *want* to be at the Playboy Club, I could have said, "No". But do we feel we *ought* to be at the Playboy Club – then my answer is "Yes, we feel we ought to be there".'

He looked at me so kindly. 'Thank you, Captain. That is all I need to know,' he said. Then he stood, shook my hand warmly and I left!

A short time later I learned that our proposed visit to the USA became questionable because USA officers and Salvationists were more than a little disturbed about our performance in the Playboy Club, when the news and photographs reached them via the media. It was then that General Coutts came personally to champion our cause, declaring quite categorically to US colleagues, 'Cancel their US tour; the Joystrings exist for the sinners, not the saints!' We couldn't have put it better ourselves.

Needless to say, we made some wonderful contacts in the club, proving that at that moment the Playboy Club was exactly where we needed to be! I am glad I was dragged out of bed early that morning to give confirmation of the rightness of our ministry at that time. Yes, it was a difficult assignment, one none of us would have chosen, but down through the years Salvationists have never chosen to go only where they have felt comfortable in sharing the gospel, and we were only going where our forebears sometimes very painfully have gone before. Our Founder would have gone!

Through it all I was encouraged when people bothered to write and let me know what had happened within their own lives or in the lives of others who had attended our concerts. Often we were made only too aware of people's disapproval of what we were doing, so that when a letter arrived telling of life-changing decisions which had been made, I rejoiced. Here is an extract from one such letter:

At the Council of Churches Annual meeting this Wednesday, the Rev Epps of Wimborne Minster said,

'I felt right from the commencement that with these beautiful young people – the Joystrings – Christ our Lord was in the midst.'

We thank you and all the members of the group for spending yourselves in abandoned and dedicated service for Christ and his Kingdom.
Brigadier Horace Foster

I must say, I did often wonder why was it that a minister from such an important church could read us so well when many of our own people could not!

One of my prayers for this book is that it will show quite definitively that although the members of the Joystrings were all young and untried, what has proved to be a monumental pivotal adventurous Christian ministry was dropped on our shoulders and had immediate effect!

It will certainly bear witness to the fact that when the Holy Spirit decides it is time for something special to happen, no one can be sure in whose direction he will choose to move or how! As I look at today's frightening and confusing world it is almost possible to hear once again William Booth's powerful words to his son Bramwell – 'Go and do something!' – ringing through the early 21st century malaise of many disadvantaged youngsters existing in a society that often fails to give them any incentive towards high moral standards of behaviour, let alone point them in the direction of religious belief.

I also pray that this book will encourage young Christians to believe that stepping out in faith is both possible and effective – even when you are learning as you go along. We are all aware that music still plays a very big part in many people's lives. Different kinds of music, naturally – but I have become convinced that any really effective music outreach from Christian young folk will only develop when they look directly at their own generation. They need to emerge from living inside the comfort zone of 'worship' songs which, beautiful though many of them are, do not address the needs of their contemporaries who are today's version of the 'swinging Sixties'. I feel this need so keenly, and this book will tell you it takes everything you have to give… and so much more!

The last time the Joystrings sang together – Peter, Bill, Wycliffe, Sylvia and me – was at the Royal Albert Hall in London in June 2004 on the occasion of the celebration of 125 years of Salvation Army music. Our appearance on that occasion had been kept secret and was an absolute surprise to practically everyone gathered. When we had finished singing our spot of two songs, during which people were on their feet singing along with us and many were in tears with the emotion of it all, we turned to exit the stage but were told by the ushers instead to remain where we were. As we turned back to face the vast audience, I saw a flag being carried on to the stage, followed by Commissioner Shaw Clifton, who at that time was the Territorial Commander for the UK (later he became General). I thought then, 'How lovely – he knows this is the last time we shall ever sing together and he is going to ask God's blessing on us.' Suddenly he took my arm and I sensed this was not what I had assumed it to be. Then I heard him begin to read something that sounded like a citation. Around me I could hear whispers of the words 'Order of the Founder', and I remember thinking, 'I have never heard of this honour being conferred upon members of a group before.' And then it finally dawned – what was being read was personal to my life and not the life of the Joystrings. Then the medal was duly pinned to my uniform. I just remember the roar of applause from those present and the other Joystrings members around me congratulating me. Every photo taken of me on that occasion shows my mouth open in amazement – not too flattering, actually, but much in harmony with what I was feeling at the time!

If I am honest, I still wish it had been possible for the Order of the Founder to have been given in such a way that embraced everyone who was part of Joystrings or who worked with us in a supporting role. I suppose that's asking for the impossible, but I am profoundly grateful and will never forget any of them.

Since then I have learned from Salvation Army history that at that time I was only the fourth officer to have received this Order in connection with service given to Christian arts and music. I was so grateful that this was quickly followed the next year by the recognition of the life and service of my fellow-officer musician and dear friend, Lieut-Colonel Ray Steadman Allen. I am sure he was similarly astonished.

The next day following the Royal Albert Hall performance, at the music leaders' councils which were held at our beloved training college at Denmark Hill where the Joystrings came to birth, I had the opportunity to kneel at that most hallowed place – the mercy seat, where as a young fledgling cadet I had signed my officer's covenant. On this day I said 'Yes' again to that all-embracing call which Catherine Bramwell Booth had reminded me of in her letter years previously and which had supported and encouraged us throughout the Joystrings years.

As I write, I am conscious that this book would never have been envisaged, even as a possibility, were it not for the original inspiration of its writer, Sylvia. She has relentlessly driven herself to explore every avenue of source material, every possibility of photo additions – in fact all that contributes to making it a fitting record of an inspirational period in the history of The Salvation Army. I am also aware that before this book was envisioned we actually merited just two small sentences in the officially recorded history of The Salvation Army. Therefore I want to thank Sylvia for her meticulous research and hours of work which together with her husband Peter's constant support has resulted in the accurate and dynamic record it has become.

I conclude with the words of the first verse of a song I wrote for Pauline and Keith's wedding. They were the desire of all of us, as the Joystrings sang for them during their wedding service, and they remain our promise for the future.

This day, this time
Thine own shall be.
And all the days ahead
We promise Thee!
And all the glory shall be Thine,
Yes! All the glory shall be Thine!

Joy Webb, Major, OF

143

144

The Joystrings + 1

INDEX